Food 4 Osteoporosis

Four Week Eating Plan

Volume 1
First Edition

Fight Osteoporosis with Food

By Nancy Robinson, Registered Dietitian Nutritionist

Contents

Introduction

The Primary Goal of the Food 4 Osteoporosis Four Week Eating Plan is to provide your bones with nutrients from meals that contain lots of fruits and vegetables and only moderate amounts of meat and cheese. A high vegetable and fruit intake provides micronutrients that are essential for bone formation. Fruits and vegetables contain more of the key nutrients necessary for bone strength than animal foods. Vegetable intake is key to obtaining Calcium from a variety of plant sources. Vegetables and fruits also reduce the acid load of the diet.

A large number of studies show that as fruit and vegetable consumption increases so does bone density. It is possible that fruits and vegetables are beneficial to bone health through yet to be discovered mechanisms. Amy Joy Lanou, Ph.D. and Michael Castleman in their book "Building Bone Vitality" reviewed 103 studies on the bone mineral density effects of fruits and vegetables or studies of nutrients found mainly in fruits and vegetables. Eighty four percent of the studies found that with an increase in fruit, vegetable or anti-oxidant intake bone mineral density also increased. Nine percent of the studies were inconclusive and only 7 percent showed no effect on bone mineral density from fruits and vegetables.

In addition to being crucial for healthy bones, a liberal fruit and vegetable intake may also reduce your risk of developing other diseases such as Cancer, Diabetes, Heart Disease and Alzheimer's.

Beverages
You can drink coffee or tea on the Eating Plan but it is recommended that you limit servings to one to two cups (caffeinated or decaffeinated) per day if not contraindicated for other health reasons. Some studies have shown that excess intake of coffee seems to increase renal calcium loss. However, another study concluded 1 to 2 cups of coffee per day has little impact on calcium loss.

Herbal teas, Rooibos tea and Hibiscus tea are good beverage choices. Water with lemon/lime juice or mineral water is great for adding alkalinity to the diet. It is also recommended that you avoid soft drinks, diet or regular, and other sweetened beverages. Be sure to drink lots of fluids throughout the day.

Substitutions

In order to take advantage of local and seasonal availability and variety as well as personal food preferences you can substitute different fruits and vegetables for the fruits and vegetables specified in the Eating plan. You can always eat more vegetables.

The Eating Plan is designed to start on a Monday (Day 1) and have the more time consuming recipes on the weekend however you can switch the days around and repeat days if you don't like the Eating plan for a particular day. You can switch the Lunch and Dinner. If you don't want to cook every day then on some days make enough for more than one day and eat leftovers.

Acid Load

Each day's menu includes enough bone healthy fruits and vegetables to balance out the high acid foods in that day's menu. A popular theory related to Osteoporosis and diet is that the higher the acid load or acid producing potential of your diet the more acidic your blood becomes resulting in bone loss and muscle wasting. This is considered an even more significant issue in older people because of declining kidney function. The theory proposes that the body tries to defend against increasing acid by breaking down bone and muscle. Some scientists believe dietary acid loads from Western diets may be a risk factor for Osteoporosis. The acid load of a particular food is determined by what the food releases into the bloodstream upon metabolism not on the acidity of the food prior to metabolism. Grains like breads, cereals, rice, and pasta as well as meat, fish, egg yolks and cheeses release acids into the bloodstream upon metabolism. Fruits and vegetables break down to add alkali (opposite of acid) to the bloodstream which helps neutralize acid. Sugars and fats are generally neutral. Foods with higher acid loads, such as cheese and meat, don't have to be eliminated from the diet but they need to be eaten in moderation and correctly balanced with alkaline foods so the net effect is a more alkaline, bone healthy diet.

Research indicates the best way to reduce dietary acid load is to eat lots of fruits and vegetables with modest amounts of breads, cereals and pastas and adequate protein but not excessive animal protein.

Follow my Blog at www.food4osteoporosis.com for updates on studies and new information related to the Osteoporosis Acid Load theory.

Calcium

Each day's menu has approximately 1200 milligrams of Calcium. If you follow the menu plan it is not necessary or beneficial to take a Calcium supplement. If you want to avoid dairy products then use a non-dairy yogurt when yogurt is included on the menu. Use a yogurt product with 300 milligrams Calcium per 8 ounce serving. Calcium absorption is highest in amounts less than 500 milligrams of Calcium at one time which is why the Eating Plan often has you divide the smoothies in half so that you drink them at two different times of the day.

It is definitely important that we all get adequate Calcium however recent studies have questioned the safety of taking large doses of Calcium supplements. The results of studies dealing with the risks and positive effects of Calcium have been very inconsistent however they do seem to indicate that getting all your Calcium as one or two large doses of a supplement is not the way the body is designed to absorb Calcium and is not the same as getting your Calcium from food. So with Calcium more may not be better. Calcium from supplements may increase the risk of cardiovascular disease and kidney stones if you get too much Calcium from supplements or if you already get enough Calcium from your diet and take supplemental Calcium. Calcium supplements are thought to cause blood Calcium levels to increase much more abruptly than Calcium rich foods. Mark Hegsted, a long time Harvard nutrition researcher, who died in 2009 at age 95, suggested that very high Calcium intakes consumed for many years impaired the body's ability to regulate Calcium resulting in a disruption of calcium absorption and excretion.

Regarding the increased risk of cardiovascular disease due to Calcium supplements, the theory has been proposed that giving large amounts of Calcium as supplements at one time may be facilitating the development of calcifications in the arteries. In the

Women's Health Initiative study the women consuming more Calcium from their diets were less likely to develop kidney stones so dietary Calcium may act differently in regard to kidney stone formation than Calcium supplements. Since Calcium from food is absorbed at a slower rate than from supplements and usually in smaller amounts at this point it seems safest to get your Calcium from food instead of supplements.

Some research suggests that it may be healthier to get Calcium from a variety of plant foods because they contain other important bone building nutrients. While Calcium is necessary to good bone health, the strength of your bones depends more on everything you eat and how active you are than just how much Calcium you consume.

Countries with the highest consumption of Milk, Dairy and Calcium have the world's highest fracture rates. Many non-western countries with the lowest fracture rates and Osteoporosis consume less Calcium than western countries (400 to 600 milligrams per day). Explanations for this "Calcium Paradox" may relate to what else these populations are consuming in their diets and the significant differences between western and non-western diets in intakes of processed foods, sodium, meat, dairy, fruits and vegetables.

Salt/Sodium
Your use of salt should be determined according to your specific situation. The sodium content of the menus is approximately 1500 milligrams per day to accommodate individuals needing or wanting to limit sodium intake. If the menu is below 1500 milligrams for that particular day the plan will tell you how much additional salt you can add to food that day and still be within 1500 milligrams sodium. Each daily menu also states how much additional salt you can add to food and not exceed 2300 milligrams per day.

High sodium/salt intakes may be a risk factor for numerous health conditions. The Dietary Guidelines for Americans recommends limiting sodium to less than 2300 milligrams per day or 1500 milligrams if you are 51 years or older, if you are Black or you have high blood pressure, diabetes or chronic kidney disease. The American Heart Association recommends 1500 mg. sodium per day. Each 1/8 teaspoon of salt added in cooking or directly to food adds

291 milligrams of sodium.   A few studies have investigated the effect of sodium on bone density. The results have been mixed with some indicating a high salt diet reduces bone density and some finding no effect on bone density. One of the main sources of sodium in the American diet is processed food. Restaurant food can also be a significant source of sodium.

Calories

All daily menus contain approximately 1600 calories to accommodate individuals trying to lose or maintain their weight. If you are not trying to lose weight or restrict your calories to 1600 per day then you can use more of the heart healthy fats such as olive oil, almond butter, avocado and nuts, however you should still limit these fats to moderate amounts. You can also be more generous with the salad dressings, eat more fruits and vegetables or add more fruits or vegetables to the Smoothies. You can add a few squares of a high cocoa content chocolate bar for dessert. Try to go with an 85% or higher cocoa content and preferably not one containing additives such as soy.   Each day's menu outlines additional food options specific to that day for those not limiting calories to 1600 per day. The sodium level will go up with the extra food so if you are limiting sodium you may need to decrease salt with the larger portion sizes.

When restricted to 1600 calories the Eating Plan does not contain enough calories for pregnant or lactating women or for growing children.

With daily exercise and moderate sensible eating most people should be able to stay at a healthy weight. When you occasionally overeat or overindulge in high calorie foods either adjust your eating afterward to compensate or plan ahead by cutting back on some other food. Read food labels and learn where excess calories slip in and how to compensate without sacrificing good nutrition. Calorie counting does work as a weight loss strategy but as one transitions from weight loss mode to weight maintenance mode it is much more enjoyable to exercise daily and practice moderation and restraint in eating rather than worrying with counting calories.

Protein
The menus average 75 to 80 grams protein per day. Individuals with conditions or diseases affecting protein metabolism or with unique dietary needs should work closely with a Registered Dietitian specializing in that condition for individualized dietary guidance and counseling.

Fat
The fat content of the menus is low to moderate depending on the day and predominately from food containing heart healthy fats such as olive oil, fish, nuts, almond butter and avocado. Cheese and meat servings are small in size to limit unhealthy fats and acid load yet still allow enjoyment of these foods.

Fiber
The menus are high in fiber, which is good for digestive and heart health and may facilitate weight loss by filling you up and keeping you from feeling hungry. You need to drink plenty of fluids when consuming a high fiber diet. If you currently do not eat a high fiber diet you should transition yourself gradually on to the high fiber intake to avoid bloating, gas or discomfort as your body adjusts to the higher fiber intake.

Choosing whole grain bread or crackers
Manufacturers must list their ingredients in descending order, so the first few ingredients are key. When purchasing whole grain breads, crackers or chips the word "whole" should be on the ingredient list. The first ingredient should be "whole wheat flour" or whatever whole grains the product contains. The terms "stone ground", "cracked wheat", "multigrain", "whole grain", "wheat or wheat flour" do not prove the product is 100% whole grain. If a product has the 100% Whole Grains Stamp on it then all its grain ingredients are whole grains. Even if it is 100% whole grains, it can still contain high fructose corn syrup or be high in sugar or hydrogenated fat so look for these ingredients as well. Also be sure the label does not include a long list of additives. Usually, a good guideline is the fewer ingredients, the better.

Other considerations
If you are accustomed to eating high fat, high sodium processed foods or very few fruits and vegetables then you may find that you

need to give yourself some time to adjust to a different and healthier way of eating. If you stick with it you will come to appreciate the greater variety of flavors and positive experiences of eating nutritious, real food that is good for your bones, body and mind.

If you take the anticoagulant warfarin and the Food 4 Osteoporosis Eating Plan is higher in vegetables, especially kale and other green leafy vegetables, than you are used to eating, then work with your Health Care Provider to monitor and adjust your medication as appropriate.

If you are a menstruating woman then the diet may not meet your iron requirements and you should discuss the use of an iron supplement with your Health Care Provider. An iron supplement should not be necessary, and in general is not recommended due to possible adverse effects of excess iron, for women no longer menstruating or for men unless you have a unique health situation warranting iron supplementation.

The Eating Plan is not a substitute for individualized care by a Physician.   Individuals with additional health challenges and complications including, but not limited to diabetes, kidney disease, cancer, irritable bowel syndrome or celiac disease should work directly with a Registered Dietitian that specializes in these conditions.

Don't Forget the Primary Goal of the Eating Plan is to provide your bones with nutrients from meals that contain lots of fruits and vegetables and only moderate amounts of meat and cheese.

To download the weekly grocery list as a PDF or Excel file that you can further customize to your own shopping needs go to **www.food4osteoporosis.com/grocery-lists.html** or download on your Smartphone.

For more information on fighting Osteoporosis with Food, when future volumes of the Four Week Eating Plans will be available and to follow my Blog go to **www.food4osteoporosis.com**

If you have suggestions for improving future Eating Plan volumes or other input regarding how the Food 4 Osteoporosis Four Week Eating Plans can help you fight Osteoporosis I welcome and appreciate your ideas which can be communicated to me at **nancy@food4osteoporosis.com**

Day 1 Menu

Breakfast
Almond Toast
Greek Yogurt with Raspberries
Beverage of Choice

Lunch
Farro Kale Salad
½ of Cherry Smoothie
Orange
Beverage of Choice

Snack anytime during the Day
Other half of Cherry Smoothie

Dinner
Chicken Fajitas
Pico de gallo and Avocado
Beverage of Choice

Salt/Sodium for the Day: If you are limiting sodium to 1500 mg./day then leave the salt out of the Farro Kale Salad (tortillas use up a lot of the sodium for the day so if you use low sodium whole grain tortillas or corn tortillas you can still use the salt in the salad). If limiting to 2300 mg/day you can add an additional 1/4 tsp. salt to food or in cooking today beyond what is already in the recipes.

Calories for the Day: If not restricting calories to 1600 per day you have the options of having a second Almond Toast at Breakfast, having a larger portion of the Farro Kale Salad at Lunch, and additional avocado or guacamole at Dinner.

Recipes:
Breakfast: Almond Toast with Raspberries and Greek yogurt.

Per person:
Spread 2 Tbsp. almond butter on 1 slice toasted whole grain bread.
Mix ½ cup raspberries with ½ cup Plain Nonfat Greek Yogurt and 1
tsp. honey.

Lunch: Farro Kale Salad, ½ Cherry Smoothie.

Cherry Smoothie recipe: To be divided to drink ½ at Lunch, ½ as
snack anytime during the day.

Blend all of the following ingredients in a high-speed blender until
smooth:
1 cup unsweetened Almond Milk (Calcium calculation based on
    using almond milk containing 300 mg Calcium per 8 ounces or
    30% of the Calcium RDA. If using a product higher than 300 mg.
    then use only amount of Almond Milk required for 300 mg.
    Calcium and use water for the rest of the liquid).
1/2 cup plain nonfat Greek Yogurt (containing 300 mg Calcium per 1
    cup serving. Nutrition label will say 30% of the RDA for Calcium)
1 cup frozen cherries
1 cup frozen beets
1 cup kale
1 medium banana
1 Tbsp. flaxseed (optional, just adds 37 calories and has lots of
    health benefits)

Add additional water or ice cubes if a different consistency is
desired.
If you have parsley or other greens that you need to use before they
go bad then add them to your smoothie – don't let them go to waste.

Farro Kale Salad recipe: Serves 4 (make enough for lunch on Day 3, too)

Preheat oven to 400° F.

1 cup farro, rinsed
2 cups cherry tomatoes
¼ cup red onion, chopped
1 tsp. olive oil
2 cups shredded fresh curly kale (or baby kale)
¼ cup flat leaf or Italian Parsley, chopped
¼ cup fresh squeezed lemon juice
¼ tsp. sea salt
¼ tsp. black pepper or to taste
¼ cup feta cheese
¼ cup sunflower seeds

Cook farro according to package directions. Drain any excess water and let cool slightly.

In small bowl combine cherry tomatoes, onion and olive oil. Spread on parchment lined baking sheet and cook at 400° for 20 minutes or until tomatoes pop.

In medium bowl combine farro, tomato onion mixture, kale, parsley, lemon juice, salt and pepper.

Top each serving with 1 Tbsp. feta cheese and 1 Tbsp. sunflower seeds.

Dinner: 2 Chicken Fajitas

Grill, or prepare as desired, 3 ounces chicken per person. Season chicken with chili powder, paprika, onion powder, garlic powder, cumin and cayenne pepper. Divide 3 ounces grilled chicken per person into 2 whole grain tortillas with 1 Tbsp. cheddar cheese in each tortilla (2 Tbsp. total per person), as much Pico de Gallo as you want, and ¼ cup avocado wedges or guacamole.

Pico de Gallo:
2 Tbsp. chopped Cilantro
2 Tbsp. chopped onion
1 Jalapeno, chopped finely
½ cup chopped tomato
1 clove garlic, minced

For Pico de Gallo: In small bowl mix cilantro, onion, jalapeno, tomato and garlic.

Guacamole Recipe:

1 ripe avocado
1 tsp. Lime juice
1 green onion, chopped
1 Tbsp. cilantro, chopped
¼ small tomato, chopped
1 clove garlic, minced
1/8 tsp. sea salt
black pepper to taste
chopped jalapeno to taste (optional)

Cut avocados in half working around seed. Remove seed. Scoop out avocado from the peel, and put in a mixing bowl. Mash avocado with fork and mix in lime juice, green onion, cilantro, tomato, garlic, sea salt, black pepper and jalapeno pepper, if desired. Adjust seasonings to taste. Serve immediately.

Day 2 Menu

<u>Breakfast</u>
Granola with Peaches or Fruit of Choice
Beverage of Choice

<u>Snack anytime during the day</u>
½ of Strawberry Smoothie

<u>Lunch</u>
Hummus
Broccoli & Cauliflower
Whole Grain Crackers or Bread
Apple or other fruit of choice
Other ½ Strawberry Smoothie
Beverage of Choice

<u>Dinner</u>
Shrimp Vegetable Stir Fry
Brown Rice
Mixed Greens Salad with Parsley Dill Dressing
Beverage of Choice

Salt/Sodium for the Day: If you are limiting sodium to 1500 mg./day then you should not add salt to food or in cooking today beyond what is already in the recipes. If limiting to 2300 mg/day you can add an additional 3/8 tsp. salt to food or in cooking today OR you can use tamari or soy sauce on the Shrimp Stir Fry not to exceed 850 mg sodium in a serving.

Calories for the Day: If not restricting calories to 1600 per day you have the options of   more Granola with fruit at Breakfast, a larger portion of Hummus and vegetables at Lunch, more salad and dressing at Dinner and 1 slice whole grain bread or roll at Dinner.

Recipes

Breakfast: ½ cup Granola with ¾ cup Non-fat Plain Greek Yogurt, ½ cup peaches and 1 tsp. honey or maple syrup if desired. May substitute unsweetened Almond Milk or a non-dairy yogurt for Greek Yogurt. May substitute another fruit for Peaches. You will need to make the Granola before the morning you plan to eat it. Store it for future use.

Granola Recipe: Makes approximately 12 cups of Granola.

Preheat oven to 300° F.

½ cup Canola Oil (preferably non GMO)
½ cup honey
½ cup maple syrup
½ cup smooth peanut butter
6 ounces prune juice
1 ½ tsp. ground cinnamon
¼ tsp. ground cloves
1 ½ tsp. ground ginger

Mix the above ingredients well in a blender.

In a large bowl mix:
4 cups of rolled oats (not instant)
2 cups wheat bran (may substitute oat bran)
½ cup chopped pecans
½ cup pecan halves
1 cup sliced almonds
1 cup whole cashews

Add ingredients from blender (oil, honey etc.) to oat, bran and nut mixture. Mix until well coated.

Line 2 metal baking pans (approx.19x12x1¼ inches each) with parchment paper. Divide the granola equally between the 2 pans, spreading it in a single layer on the pans. Cook for approximately 1 hour at 300° F., stirring every 15 to 20 minutes. Once the granola is golden brown remove from the oven. Cool and store in an airtight container.

½ as Snack and ½ at Lunch: Strawberry Smoothie. May substitute another fruit for Strawberries.

Strawberry Smoothie Recipe: To be divided to drink half at lunch and half as snack anytime during the day.

Per person blend all of the following ingredients in a high-speed blender until smooth:
1 ¼ cups unsweetened Almond Milk (Calcium calculation based on
   using almond milk containing 300 mg Calcium per 8 ounces or
   30% of the Calcium RDA. If using a product higher than 300 mg.
   then use only amount of Almond Milk required for 300 mg.
   Calcium and use water for the rest of the liquid).
1/4 cup plain nonfat Greek Yogurt (containing 300 mg Calcium per 1
   cup serving. Nutrition label will say 30% of the RDA for Calcium)
1 cup raw kale
1 cup frozen or fresh strawberries (may substitute another fruit for
   strawberries)
1 medium banana
1 Tbsp. flaxseed (optional, just adds 37 calories and has lots of
   health benefits)

Add additional water or ice cubes if a different consistency is desired.
If you have parsley or other greens that you need to use before they go bad then add them to your smoothie – don't let them go to waste.

Lunch: 1/2 cup Hummus with raw Broccoli (as much as you like) and Cauliflower (as much as you like) plus 6 whole grain crackers or a slice of whole grain bread (I like Flackers – crackers made from flax seeds or try Multigrain Wasa Flatbreads). Apple or other fruit of choice. One half Strawberry Smoothie.

Dinner: Shrimp Vegetable Stir Fry with Brown Rice, Mixed Greens Salad with Parsley Dill Dressing.

Cook brown rice (1 cup cooked per person) while preparing Shrimp Stir Fry and Salad. I prefer Basmati brown rice.

Shrimp Vegetable Stir Fry Recipe: Makes 4 servings (1/2 recipe for 2)

1 Tbsp. olive oil
4 garlic cloves, finely diced
2 sweet red peppers, seeded and cut julienne
1 large onion, thinly sliced
4 cups broccoli, cut into bite sized pieces
2 Tbsp. toasted unsalted pine nuts
2 Tbsp. raisins
12 ounces medium shrimp, cooked, shelled and deveined
1/8 tsp. sea salt
freshly ground pepper, to taste

Heat olive oil in wok or large skillet over medium heat. Add garlic and cook, stirring constantly, until golden, about 1 minute. Remove garlic from pan and reserve. Add red pepper and onion and stir fry until slightly softened about 3 to 4 minutes. Mix in broccoli, pine nuts and raisins and stir-fry until broccoli is crisp tender, about 2 minutes. Return garlic to pan along with shrimp and stir-fry just until heated through. Season with salt and pepper and serve immediately with 1-cup brown rice per serving.

Serve with Salad made of Mixed Greens and tomatoes. Use ½ cup cherry or sliced tomatoes and at least 1 cup mixed greens (may use more than 1 cup) per person. Buy pre-packaged mixed greens or buy or grow an assortment of different salad greens like arugula, mache, dandelion, and assorted lettuces. Allow ¼ cup Parsley Dill dressing per salad.

Parsley Dill Salad Dressing Recipe: Makes 1 cup dressing

¾ cup Fat Free Plain Greek Yogurt
½ cup minced flat leaf parsley
2 Tbsp. minced red onion
2 Tbsp. fresh dill or 1 tsp. dried dill
2 Tbsp. lemon juice
1 tsp. 100% maple syrup
1/8 tsp. salt
2 Tbsp. olive oil
Mix all ingredients in a blender. Blend until smooth. Refrigerate.

Day 3 Menu

Breakfast
**Almond Toast
Greek Yogurt with Strawberries
Beverage of Choice**

Snack anytime during the Day
½ Pineapple Smoothie

Lunch
**Farro Kale Salad
Other ½ of Pineapple Smoothie
Beverage of Choice**

Dinner
**Vegetable Roast
Blueberry "It's not really Ice Cream"
Beverage of Choice**

Salt/Sodium for the Day: If you are limiting sodium to 1500 mg./day then you can add 1/8 tsp. salt to food or in cooking today beyond what is already in the recipes. If limiting to 2300 mg/day you can add an additional 1/2 tsp. salt to food or in cooking today beyond what is already in the recipes or use Tamari or soy sauce on the Vegetable Roast (not to exceed 1163 mg. sodium in the soy sauce serving).

Calories for the Day: If not restricting calories to 1600 per day you have the options of having a second Almond Toast at Breakfast, having all the Farro Kale Salad at Lunch that you want, and all you want of the Vegetable Roast and Blueberry dessert at Dinner. You can also have a serving of whole grain bread at both Lunch and Dinner.

Recipes:

Breakfast: Almond Toast with Strawberries and Greek yogurt.

Per person:
Spread 2 Tbsp. almond butter on 1 slice toasted whole grain bread.
Mix ½ cup strawberries with ½ cup Plain Nonfat Greek Yogurt and 1
tsp. honey.

½ as Snack and ½ at Lunch: Pineapple Smoothie. May substitute
another fruit for Pineapple.

Pineapple Smoothie Recipe: To be divided to drink half at lunch
and half as snack anytime during the day.

Per person blend all of the following ingredients in a high-speed
blender until smooth:
¾ cups of unsweetened Almond Milk (Calcium calculation based
   on using almond milk containing 300 mg Calcium per 8 ounces
   or 30% of the Calcium RDA. If using a product higher than 300
   mg. then use only amount of Almond Milk required for 300 mg.
   Calcium and use water for the rest of the liquid).
½ cup plain nonfat Greek Yogurt (containing 300 mg Calcium per 1
   cup serving. Nutrition label will say 30% of the RDA for Calcium)
1 ½ cups raw kale
1 cup frozen, canned or fresh pineapple (may substitute another
   fruit for pineapple)
1 medium banana
1 Tbsp. flaxseed (optional, just adds 37 calories and has lots of
   health benefits)

Add additional water or ice cubes if a different consistency is
desired.
If you have parsley or other greens that you need to use before they
go bad then add them to your smoothie – don't let them go to waste.

Lunch: Farro Kale Salad (leftover from Day 1), ½ Pineapple
Smoothie.

Dinner: Vegetable Roast, Blueberry "It's not really Ice Cream".

Vegetable Roast Recipe: Makes 4 servings (Make enough for leftovers for lunch tomorrow)

Preheat oven to 400° F.

4 cups cooked brown basmati rice
¼ tsp. sea salt
½ tsp. coriander, ground
¼ tsp. ginger, ground

½ tsp. red pepper flakes
½ tsp. ground coriander
1 tsp. curry powder
½ tsp. ground ginger
½ tsp. crushed mustard seeds
2 Tbsp. fresh oregano, chopped or 1 tsp. dried
½ tsp. garlic powder
¼ tsp. sea salt
2 cups cauliflower, cut into bite size pieces
2 cups broccoli, cut into bite size pieces
1 fennel bulb, sliced into bite size pieces
1 cup red bell pepper, cut into bite size pieces
1 cup yellow bell pepper, cut into bite size pieces
1 cup onion, cut into bite size pieces
20 cherry tomatoes
2 Tbsp. olive oil
1 15 oz. cans No salt added Garbanzo Beans (Chick Peas) or 2
    cups cooked garbanzo beans I like Eden No Salt Added canned
    beans with BPA free lining or try Whole Foods 365 Organic No
    salt added beans that are packed in cartons. If you have time
    cook your own from dried beans.
¼ cup chopped flat leaf parsley

Prepare basmati rice according to package directions. Add ¼ tsp. salt, ½ tsp. coriander and ¼ tsp. ginger to cooking water.

In small bowl mix red pepper, coriander, curry, ginger, mustard seeds, oregano, garlic powder and ¼ tsp. salt. Set aside.

In large bowl mix cauliflower, broccoli, fennel, red bell pepper, yellow bell pepper, onion and cherry tomatoes. Add olive oil to vegetables mixing to coat all vegetables with oil. Add the spice mixture to the vegetables and mix to coat all vegetables.

Distribute vegetables evenly on a baking sheet lined with parchment paper. Cook at 400° F. for 20 to 25 minutes or until tomatoes pop and vegetables are starting to just brown. Remove from oven and add garbanzo beans to pan, mixing beans into vegetables and turning vegetables. Cook another 5 minutes. Serve over rice. Top with parsley.

Optional if you can afford the calories and/or sodium:
Serve with low sodium Tamari sauce. Also good topped with almonds, raisins or dried apricots. Or drizzle a high quality olive oil over the top.

Blueberry "Not Really Ice Cream" Recipe:
For each serving combine 1 cup blueberries, ¼ cup yogurt and 2 tsp. 100% maple syrup in a food processor or blender. Blend until smooth. Serve immediately or put it in the freezer for a few minutes if you want a firmer consistency.

Day 4 Menu

Breakfast
Oatmeal with Blueberries and Walnuts
½ of Mango Smoothie
Beverage of Choice

Lunch
Vegetable Roast
Other ½ of Mango Smoothie
Beverage of Choice

Dinner
Salmon with Whole Grain Mustard
Roasted Cauliflower
Wheat and Barley Pilaf
Beverage of Choice

Salt/Sodium for the Day: If you are limiting sodium to 1500 mg./day then you should not add additional salt to food or in cooking today beyond what is already in the recipes. If limiting to 2300 mg/day you can add an additional 3/8 tsp. salt to food or in cooking today.

Calories for the Day: If not restricting calories to 1600 per day you have the options of having more Oatmeal and fruit at Breakfast, all you want of the Vegetable Roast at Lunch, more cauliflower at Dinner, more olive oil on your Cauliflower and Wheat and Barley Bowl and 2 oz. more Salmon at Dinner.

Recipes

Breakfast: Steel Cut Oatmeal with Blueberries & Walnuts, ½ of Mango Smoothie

Oatmeal recipe: Makes 1 serving.

¼ cup steel cut oats (may substitute rolled oats if you prefer)
1 cup unsweetened almond milk
1/4 tsp. ground cinnamon, or to taste
1/8 tsp. ground ginger, or to taste
1/2 tsp. vanilla, or to taste
1 tsp. honey or maple syrup
1 Tbsp. flaxseed (optional, just adds 37 calories and has lots of
    health benefits)
½ cup blueberries
1 Tbsp. walnuts, chopped

Prepare oatmeal according to package directions using almond milk instead of water. Mix in cinnamon, ginger, vanilla, honey (or maple syrup) and flaxseed. Once cooked to desired consistency add blueberries and walnuts and serve immediately.

Mango Smoothie recipe: To be divided to drink ½ at breakfast and ½ at lunch.

Blend all of the following ingredients in a high-speed blender until smooth:
1 cup of unsweetened Almond Milk (Calcium calculation based on
    using almond milk containing 300 mg Calcium per 8 ounces or
    30% of the Calcium RDA. If using a product higher than 300 mg.
    then use only amount of Almond Milk required for 300 mg.
    Calcium and use water for the rest of the liquid).
1/2 cup plain nonfat Greek Yogurt (containing 300 mg Calcium per 1
    cup serving. Nutrition label will say 30% of the RDA for Calcium)
1 cup raw kale
1 cup frozen or fresh mango (may substitute another fruit for
    mango)
1 medium banana
1 Tbsp. flaxseed (optional, just adds 37 calories and has lots of
    health benefits)

Add additional water or ice cubes if a different consistency is desired.

If you have parsley or other greens that you need to use before they go bad then add them to your smoothie – don't let them go to waste.

Lunch: Vegetable Roast leftover from yesterday, other 1/2 of Mango Smoothie.

Dinner: Salmon, Roasted Cauliflower and Wheat and Barley Pilaf. Cook extra 4 ounces salmon per person for lunch salad tomorrow.

Salmon Recipe:
Preheat oven to 400° F. if not grilling salmon.

4 ounces raw salmon (preferably wild) per person plus 4 ounces raw
   salmon per person for lunch salad tomorrow
1 Tbsp. whole grain mustard per person
½ cup white wine or water if not grilling

Spread mustard on raw salmon.   Cook on grill until just done.   Or put in baking dish, add white wine or water and bake uncovered for 12 to 15 minutes or until just done. Avoid overcooking which will dry the salmon out.   Refrigerate 4 ounces for salad tomorrow and eat the other 4 ounces for dinner.

Roasted Cauliflower Recipe: Don't just use the white, try some of the colored cauliflower and mix them for a colorful dish.

Preheat oven to 400° F.

Per person:
1 cup cauliflower, washed and cut into bite size florets
1 tsp. olive oil
1/8 tsp. kosher or sea salt
Black pepper to taste
Lemon juice/wedges, if desired

Place cauliflower in bowl. Add olive oil to coat cauliflower (if you use your hands it will coat more evenly). Add salt, pepper and any other desired herbs or spices like cardamom, red chili flakes, cilantro, coriander, cumin, curry, dill, garlic powder, paprika, saffron, thyme or turmeric.   Dill would be good with the Fish.   Evenly distribute cauliflower in a single layer on a parchment lined baking pan. Bake at 400° F. for 35 to 45 minutes or until soft and browned, stirring after 10 minutes and again as needed. If you can afford the extra calories drizzle a little high quality olive oil on the cauliflower just before serving.

Wheat and Barley Pilaf Recipe: Makes 4 servings, ½ recipe for 2.

1 cup barley
1 tsp. olive oil for cooking barley
3 cups water or 2 ½ cups water plus ½ cup white wine
½ tsp. sea salt
¼ tsp. black pepper, or more if desired
½ tsp. garlic powder
¼ tsp. smoked paprika
¼ cup bulgur or cracked wheat
6 ounces spinach, shredded or 6 cups lightly packed spinach
½ cup sliced green onions
¼ cup flat leaf parsley, chopped
Juice of 1 lemon
1 cup cherry tomatoes, cut in half
¼ cup sunflower seeds
4 tsp. high quality olive oil to drizzle over each serving (if not limiting calories to 1600)

Heat olive oil over medium heat in a large skillet. Add barley and cook until golden brown, approximately 5 minutes. Mix in water, salt, pepper, garlic powder and paprika. Bring to a boil. Reduce heat to low, cover and cook for 40 minutes. Add bulgur wheat and simmer covered another 15 minutes.

Stir in spinach, green onions, parsley, lemon juice, tomatoes and sunflower seeds. Heat until warm and serve. Drizzle 1 tsp. high quality olive oil over each serving if not limiting calories to 1600.

Day 5 Menu

<u>Breakfast</u>
Granola with Strawberries or Fruit of Choice
Beverage of Choice

<u>Snack anytime during the day</u>
Peach Smoothie

<u>Lunch</u>
Salmon Spinach Salad with Avocado Dressing
Whole Grain Roll, Bread or Crackers
Apple or other fruit of choice
Beverage of Choice

<u>Dinner</u>
Butternut Squash Quesadilla
Guacamole
Pineapple Kiwi Salad
Beverage of Choice

Salt/Sodium for the Day: If you are limiting sodium to 1500 mg./day then you should not add salt to food or in cooking today beyond what is already in the recipes. If limiting to 2300 mg/day you can add an additional 3/8 tsp. salt to food or in cooking today.

Calories for the Day: If not restricting calories to 1600 per day you have the options of having more Granola and fruit at Breakfast, 2 extra ounces of salmon and additional spinach salad and avocado dressing at Lunch and more guacamole and fruit at Dinner.

Recipes

Breakfast: ½ cup Granola with ¾ cup Non-fat Plain Greek Yogurt, ½ cup sliced strawberries and 1 tsp. honey or maple syrup if desired. May substitute unsweetened Almond Milk or a non-dairy yogurt for Greek Yogurt.   May substitute another fruit for strawberries. Granola recipe is from Day 2.

Snack anytime during the day:
Peach Smoothie recipe: Makes 1 Smoothie

Blend all of the following ingredients in a high-speed blender until smooth:
1 cup of unsweetened Almond Milk (Calcium calculation based on using almond milk containing 300 mg Calcium per 8 ounces or 30% of the Calcium RDA. If using a product higher than 300 mg. then use only amount of Almond Milk required for 300 mg. Calcium and use water for the rest of the liquid).
1/2 cup raw kale
1/2 cup frozen or fresh peach slices (may substitute another fruit for peach)
1 medium banana
1 Tbsp. flaxseed (optional, just adds 37 calories and has lots of health benefits)

Add additional water or ice cubes if a different consistency is desired.
If you have parsley or other greens that you need to use before they go bad then add them to your smoothie – don't let them go to waste.

Lunch: Salmon Spinach Salad with Avocado Dressing (if good avocados are not available to you at this time of year substitute ¼ cup of the Parsley Dill Dressing from Day 2), 1 slice of whole grain bread or roll or a serving of whole grain crackers, and 1 Apple or fruit of choice for dessert.

Salmon Salad Recipe:
For each serving mix in a salad bowl:
3 cups spinach
1 cup cherry tomato halves
½ cup sliced mushrooms
½ cup sliced cucumber

Avocado Dressing: Makes 2 cups of Dressing (can substitute
    Parsley Dill from Day 2)
Blend in food processor:
1 medium avocado (seed and skin removed)
2 Tbsp. cilantro, chopped
1 green onion, chopped
1 garlic clove, chopped
1 Tbsp. champagne vinegar (may substitute white wine vinegar)
¼ tsp. sea salt
pepper to taste
2/3 cup water

Top each serving of salad with leftover 4 ounces cooked salmon
from yesterday and ¼ cup Avocado Dressing.

Dinner: 1 Butternut Squash Quesadilla and ½ of Guacamole or ½
avocado. 1 Kiwi and 1/3 cup pineapple chunks per person.

Butternut Squash Quesadilla Recipe: Makes 3 servings.
One 10 or 12 ounce bag frozen butternut squash (you can use fresh
    but frozen works fine and is faster – you can also substitute
    baked sweet potato)
¼ tsp. ground cinnamon
¼ tsp. turmeric
Juice of 1 lime
1/2 of a 15 oz. can of No salt added White Beans (Navy, Cannellini)
    or 1 cup cooked white beans I like Eden No Salt Added canned
    beans with BPA free lining or try Whole Foods 365 Organic No
    salt added beans that are packed in cartons. If you have time
    cook your own from dried beans.
¼ cup chopped cilantro
3 green onions, chopped
1 jalapeno pepper, chopped
1/8 tsp. sea salt
6 whole grain tortillas
1 cup grated Muenster Cheese

In a medium saucepan cook butternut squash with water until
tender. Remove from heat, drain well, and return to saucepan and
mash. Mix in cinnamon, turmeric, and lime juice.

Drain beans well. In a medium bowl combine beans with cilantro, green onion, jalapeno pepper, and sea salt.

For each of 3 whole grain tortillas spread 1/3 of squash mixture over a tortilla then 1/3 of bean mixture and 1/3 cup cheese. Top with remaining 3 tortillas.

Heat grill pan or large non-stick skillet over medium high heat. Cook quesadillas for about 3 minutes or until lightly browned then turn and brown other side. Remove from pan and cut each quesadilla into 4 wedges. Serve with guacamole or sliced avocado.

Guacamole Recipe:

1 ripe avocado
1 tsp. Lime juice
1 green onion, chopped
1 Tbsp. cilantro, chopped
¼ small tomato, chopped
1 clove garlic, minced
1/8 tsp. sea salt
black pepper to taste
chopped jalapeno to taste (optional)

Cut avocados in half working around seed. Remove seed. Scoop out avocado from the peel, and put in a mixing bow. Mash avocado with fork and mix in lime juice, green onion, cilantro, tomato, garlic, sea salt, black pepper and jalapeno pepper, if desired. Adjust seasonings to taste. Serve immediately.

Pineapple Kiwi Salad: Slice 1 kiwi and mix with 1/3 cup pineapple chunks.

Day 6 Menu

Breakfast
Almond Molasses Muffins
½ of Blueberry Smoothie
Beverage of Choice

Lunch
Pasta Salad
Orange or fruit of choice
Other 1/2 of Blueberry Smoothie
Beverage of Choice

Dinner
Bison Burgers
Sweet Potato Fries
Sliced Strawberries with Balsamic Vinegar
Beverage of Choice

Salt/Sodium for the Day: If you are limiting sodium to 1500 mg./day then you should not add salt to food or in cooking today beyond what is already in the recipes. If limiting to 2300 mg/day you can add an additional 3/8 tsp. salt to food or in cooking today.

Calories for the Day: If not restricting calories to 1600 per day you have the options of having more muffins at Breakfast, extra pasta salad, a serving of whole grain bread or crackers and fruit at Lunch, mayonnaise on your burger and more sweet potato fries at Dinner.

Recipes

Breakfast: Almond Molasses Muffins (2 muffins per person) and ½ Blueberry Smoothie.   The muffins contain 154 mg of calcium per muffin and were specifically designed to make a significant contribution to the calcium needs for the day.   Many stores (Whole Foods, Trader Jo's, local Health Food Stores and larger regional grocery stores) now carry the specialty flours required for these muffins or you can order them from specialty flour companies such as Bob's Red Mill (www.bobsredmill.com)

Almond Molasses Muffins Recipe: Makes 10 muffins.   Make enough to freeze some for Breakfast next week (on Day 10).

Preheat oven to 400° F.

¼ cup teff flour
½ cup almond flour or meal
¼ cup garbanzo bean flour
¼ tsp. salt
1 tsp. baking powder
1 tsp. cinnamon
1 tsp. ginger
½ cup molasses
¼ cup plus 2 Tbsp. almond butter
1 cup almond milk (calcium level based on using one that contains
    300 mg Calcium per 8 ounces)
1 tsp. vanilla
1 Egg

In medium bowl mix teff flour, almond flour, garbanzo bean flour, salt, baking powder, cinnamon, and ginger.   In a separate small bowl mix molasses, almond butter, almond milk, vanilla and egg until well blended.   Add liquid ingredients to dry ingredients and mix well.   Divide batter evenly in 10 muffins cups.   Muffin cups will be almost full.

Bake at 400° for 20 to 25 minutes or until a toothpick inserted into muffins comes out clean.   If baking in paper muffin cups remove from pan immediately and cool on wire cooling rack.   If not using paper muffin cups let cool 5 minutes in pan and then remove and put on wire cooling rack. If you can afford the extra calories these muffins are also delicious with chopped dried or fresh figs added to them.

Blueberry Smoothie recipe: To be divided to drink ½ at breakfast and ½ at lunch.

Blend all of the following ingredients in a high-speed blender until smooth:

1/2 cup of unsweetened Almond Milk (Calcium calculation based on using almond milk containing 300 mg Calcium per 8 ounces or 30% of the Calcium RDA. If using a product higher than 300 mg. then use only amount of Almond Milk required for 300 mg. Calcium and use water for the rest of the liquid).

3/4 cup plain nonfat Greek Yogurt (containing 300 mg Calcium per 1 cup serving. Nutrition label will say 30% of the RDA for Calcium)

1 cup raw kale

1/2 cup frozen or fresh blueberries (may substitute another fruit for blueberries)

1 medium banana

1 Tbsp. flaxseed (optional, just adds 37 calories and has lots of health benefits)

Add additional water or ice cubes if a different consistency is desired.

If you have parsley or other greens that you need to use before they go bad then add them to your smoothie – don't let them go to waste.

<u>Lunch:</u> Pasta Salad and orange or fruit of choice.

Pasta Salad recipe: Makes 4 servings (make enough for Lunch tomorrow, too)

1 cup whole-wheat penne or spiral pasta, or any whole grain pasta if you prefer gluten free

1 15 oz. can No salt added white Beans, such as Navy or Cannellini, or 1 3/4 cups cooked white beans, well drained. I like Eden No Salt Added canned beans with BPA free lining or try Whole Foods 365 Organic No salt added beans that are packed in cartons. If you have time cook your own from dried beans.

1 cup, carrots sliced in to bite size pieces

2 green onions, chopped

1 cup cherry tomatoes, cut in half
1 cup kale, chopped into bite size pieces
12 artichoke hearts, cut into bite size pieces

For dressing mix until smooth:
2 Tbsp. tahini
2 Tbsp. olive oil
1 tsp. apple cider vinegar
Juice from 1 lemon
1/8 tsp. sweet paprika or to taste (I like more)
1/8 tsp. cayenne pepper or to taste (I like more)
¼ tsp. sea salt

Cook pasta according to package directions and drain well. In large bowl mix pasta, drained beans, carrots, green onions, cherry tomatoes, kale and artichoke hearts. Mix dressing ingredients together and add to pasta.

Dinner: Bison Burger with Sweet Potato Fries.

Recipe for Bison Burgers:

4 ounces ground Bison per person/burger (may substitute 95% lean, 5% fat ground beef but if you haven't tried Bison you should give it a try. Many grocery stores now carry Bison.)
1 Tbsp. Italian flat leaf parsley for every 4 ounces bison (can substitute cilantro)
1/8 tsp. fresh ground black pepper for every 4 ounces bison
1 fresh garlic clove, chopped or crushed in garlic press for every 4 ounces bison

Whole grain hamburger buns
Spinach
Tomato, sliced
Onion, sliced
Jalapeno pepper, sliced (optional)
Mustard
Canola or olive oil mayonnaise if you can afford the calories

Mix parsley (or cilantro), pepper and garlic into ground bison and shape into 4-ounce patties.
Grill outside or cook until done in skillet on stovetop. Warm whole grain hamburger buns in oven or on griddle. Add meat to warm

buns along with fresh spinach, sliced tomato, sliced onions, jalapenos (optional), mustard of choice and canola or olive oil mayonnaise if you can afford the extra calories.

For Sweet Potato Fries you can make your own with the following recipe or for an easier option use "Alexia Sweet Potato Fries with Sea Salt" which contain 140 calories per serving, no trans or saturated fat and 140 mg sodium per serving.   Go to www.alexiafoods.com for stores near you that carry the "Sweet Potato Fries with Sea Salt".

Sweet Potato Fries Recipe: Makes 4 servings.

Preheat oven to 375° F.

2 medium sweet potatoes, organic preferably
2 tsp. olive oil
¼ tsp. sea salt
1 tsp. garlic powder
1 tsp. onion powder
2 tsp. lemon rind, preferably organic

Scrub potatoes and peel if desired (you can leave peel on if organic). Slice potatoes into fries. Mix potatoes, olive oil, salt, garlic powder, onion powder and lemon rind in bowl.   Coat fries well.

Arrange potatoes in single layer on parchment paper lined baking sheet. Bake for 25 to 30 minutes at 375°.   Turn and rearrange fries half way through baking to assure even browning.

Sliced Strawberries with Balsamic Vinegar: Drizzle 1 Tbsp. good quality Balsamic Vinegar over ½ cup sliced strawberries per person.

Day 7 Menu

Breakfast
Carrot Pancakes
Beverage of Choice

Lunch
Pasta Salad
Raspberries with Yogurt
Beverage of Choice

Dinner
Swiss Chard Lasagna in Pumpkin Sauce
Mixed Greens Salad with Avocado Dressing
Beverage of Choice

Salt/Sodium for the Day: If you are limiting sodium to 1500 mg./day then you should not add salt to food or in cooking today beyond what is already in the recipes. If limiting to 2300 mg/day you can add an additional 3/8 tsp. salt to food or in cooking today.

Calories for the Day: If not restricting calories to 1600 per day you have the options of having extra pasta salad and fruit at Lunch and more salad and salad dressing at Dinner.

Recipes
Breakfast: Carrot Pancakes

Carrot Pancake Recipe:
Makes 4 servings or 8 pancakes, 2 pancakes per serving. Half the recipe for 2 people.

¾ cup whole-wheat flour
½ cup unbleached all purpose flour
¼ cup chopped walnuts
2 tsp. baking powder
1 tsp. cinnamon
¼ tsp. salt
¼ tsp. nutmeg, ground
¼ tsp. cloves, ground
¼ tsp. ginger, ground
1 Tbsp. blackstrap molasses
1 cup lowfat buttermilk
1 Tbsp. canola oil
1 ½ tsp. vanilla
2 large eggs
¼ cup applesauce
2 cups grated carrots
100% maple syrup or extra applesauce

In a large bowl combine whole-wheat flour, all purpose flour, walnuts, baking powder, cinnamon, salt, nutmeg, cloves, and ginger.

In a medium bowl combine molasses, buttermilk, canola oil, vanilla, eggs and applesauce. Mix well and add to dry ingredients. Stir until evenly distributed and moist. Fold in grated carrots.

Heat non-stick skillet or pancake griddle to medium heat. Spoon batter on to griddle. You may need to spread the batter a little with a spatula. Cook until edges are cooked and bubbles on top start to break – about 2 minutes. Carefully turn pancakes over and cook 1 minute more or until bottoms are browned.

Serve with ¼ cup 100% maple syrup per 2 pancakes. Or even better use applesauce instead of syrup on top of the pancakes.

Lunch: Pasta Salad leftover from yesterday. For dessert ¾ cup raspberries mixed with ¾ cup yogurt and 1 tsp. honey per person.

Dinner: Swiss Chard Lasagna in Pumpkin Sauce, Mixed Green Salad with Avocado Dressing.

Swiss Chard Lasagna Recipe: Makes 4 servings. Be sure making enough for lunch tomorrow, too.

Preheat oven to 350° F.

9 whole grain lasagna noodles (about 9 ounces)
8 cups raw chopped Swiss Chard
1 Tbsp. olive oil
1 15-ounce can Pumpkin
½ tsp. cinnamon, ground
1/8 tsp. turmeric
¼ tsp. ginger, ground
1 Tbsp. blackstrap molasses
2 cups water
¼ tsp. sea salt, divided
3 ounces part skim mozzarella cheese, grated
1 cup part skim ricotta cheese

In large pot cook Lasagna noodles according to package directions. Drain well and dry on paper or lint free cloth towel.

Wash chard well and cut or strip leaves from stalks into strips and chop. Heat olive oil in large pot over medium heat. Add chard leaves to pot with water from washing clinging to it. Cook until wilted and tender stirring frequently, about 5 minutes. Drain well (also good to lay it out on paper or lint free cloth towel). Add 1/8 tsp. salt to cooked chard.

To prepare sauce, in medium bowl mix pumpkin, cinnamon, turmeric, ginger, molasses, water and 1/8 tsp. salt.

To assemble put a thin layer of Pumpkin sauce in bottom of 12x9 (or something close) pan. Lay 1/3 of lasagna noodles on top of sauce. Spread ½ of ricotta cheese on noodles. Then spread ½ of chard on top of ricotta cheese and then another layer of sauce. Add another layer of 1/3 of noodles, the other ½ of ricotta cheese and chard topping it with ½ of mozzarella cheese and some more sauce. Finish with another layer of noodles and the rest of the sauce.

Bake Lasagna for 30 to 40 minutes at 350° F. Then add remaining mozzarella cheese to top and bake 5 minutes or until cheese on top is just melted. Lasagna serves up easier if you let it sit 5 minutes after removing from oven.

For Mixed Greens salad combine 2 cups mixed greens, ½ cup broccoli (in bite size pieces) and ½ cup cauliflower (in bite size pieces) per person. Serve with ¼ cup Avocado Dressing (recipe on Day 5 menu) or 2 Tbsp. Parsley Dill Dressing (recipe on Day 2).

Day 8 Menu

Breakfast
Almond Toast
Strawberry Smoothie
Beverage of Choice

Lunch
Swiss Chard Lasagna in Pumpkin Sauce
Kiwi and Greens Salad with Maple Lemon Dressing
Beverage of Choice

Dinner
Caribbean Fish
Roasted Cauliflower
Roasted Green Beans
Whole Grain Bread or Roll
Beverage of Choice

Salt/Sodium for the Day: If you are limiting sodium to 1500 mg./day then you should not add salt to food or in cooking today beyond what is already in the recipes. If limiting to 2300 mg/day you can add an additional 3/8 tsp. salt to food or in cooking today. You will probably want to use the salt on the green beans and cauliflower at Dinner.

Calories for the Day: If not restricting calories to 1600 per day you have the options of having a second Almond Toast at Breakfast, extra salad and dressing at Lunch and more vegetables with olive oil at Dinner.

Recipes

Breakfast: Almond Toast with Strawberry Smoothie.

Spread 2 Tbsp. almond butter on 1 slice toasted whole grain bread. Prepare Strawberry Smoothie.   May substitute another fruit for Strawberries.

Strawberry Smoothie recipe: Makes 1 Smoothie

Blend all of the following ingredients in a high-speed blender until smooth:

3/4 cup of unsweetened Almond Milk (Calcium calculation based on using almond milk containing 300 mg Calcium per 8 ounces or 30% of the Calcium RDA. If using a product higher than 300 mg. then use only amount of Almond Milk required for 300 mg. Calcium and use water for the rest of the liquid).

1/4 cup plain nonfat Greek Yogurt (containing 300 mg Calcium per 1 cup serving. Nutrition label will say 30% of the RDA for Calcium)

1 cup raw kale

1/2 cup frozen or fresh strawberries (may substitute another fruit for strawberries)

1 medium banana

1 Tbsp. flaxseed (optional, just adds 37 calories and has lots of health benefits)

Add additional water or ice cubes if a different consistency is desired.

If you have parsley or other greens that you need to use before they go bad then add them to your smoothie – don't let them go to waste.

Lunch: Swiss Chard Lasagna in Pumpkin Sauce, Kiwi and Greens Salad with Maple Lemon Dressing.

Lasagna is leftover from last night's dinner. For salad for each person mix 1 cup mixed greens (can have more) with 1 Kiwi (cut in to bite size pieces) and top with 2 Tbsp. Maple Lemon Dressing.

Maple Lemon Dressing Recipe:

Mix following ingredients together in a jar and shake until well blended:

2 Tbsp. maple syrup
¼ cup fresh lemon juice
1 Tbsp. Dijon Mustard
¼ cup olive oil

Dinner: Caribbean Fish, Roasted Cauliflower, Roasted Green Beans, Whole Grain Roll or Bread.

Caribbean Fish Recipe: Makes 2 servings

Preheat oven to 400°F.

Two 4 ounce fish fillets, preferably sustainable such as Arctic Char (farmed), Tilapia (Ecuador & US), Catfish (US) or Pacific Halibut (US). Go to www.seafoodwatch.org for sustainable fish purchasing guidelines. You can also look for fish with the Marine Stewardship Council Blue eco-label in your grocery store.

1 tsp. black pepper, ground
1 ½ tsp. coriander, ground
½ tsp. cinnamon, ground
½ tsp. allspice, ground
½ tsp. nutmeg, ground
¼ tsp. garlic powder
¼ tsp. onion powder
¼ tsp. cumin, ground
½ tsp. dried thyme leaves (or 1 Tbsp. fresh)
¼ tsp. ginger, ground
¼ tsp. sea salt
1 tsp. olive oil
1 Tbsp. dark rum (can substitute 1 tsp. rum extract and 2 tsp. water)
1 Tbsp. blackstrap molasses
1 Tbsp. Apple cider vinegar
1 Tbsp. lime juice
1 medium banana, just barely ripe

In small bowl, combine pepper, coriander, cinnamon, allspice, nutmeg, garlic powder, onion powder, cumin, thyme, ginger and salt. Coat top of fish fillets in spice mixture.

Heat olive oil in skillet over medium high heat. Put fish in pan spice side down and sear. Remove fish from skillet and put on slightly oiled baking sheet. Bake fillets at 400°F. for 7 to 8 minutes or until done (opaque but firm). Cooking time will depend on thickness of fillets. Do not overcook.

While fish is baking make sauce. Mix rum, molasses, vinegar and lime juice in small saucepan over low heat. Peel and slice banana into bite size slices and add to saucepan. Stir to coat bananas with sauce. Allow sauce to simmer and reduce to a glaze. Serve sauce over fish.

Roasted Cauliflower Recipe: Don't just use the white, try some of the colored cauliflower & mix them for a colorful dish.

Preheat oven to 400° F.
Per person:
1 cup cauliflower, washed and cut into bite size florets
1 tsp. olive oil
Black pepper to taste
Lemon juice/wedges, if desired

Place cauliflower in bowl. Add olive oil to coat cauliflower (if you use your hands it will coat more evenly). Add pepper and any other desired herbs or spices like cardamom, red chili flakes, cilantro, coriander, cumin, curry, dill, garlic powder, paprika, saffron, thyme or turmeric. Cumin would be good with the Fish. Evenly distribute cauliflower in a single layer on a parchment lined baking pan. Bake at 400° F. for 35 to 45 minutes or until soft and browned, stirring once after 10 minutes and again as needed. If you can afford the extra calories drizzle a little high quality olive oil on the cauliflower just before serving.

If you can find haricots verts (French Green beans that are thinner, more tender with a more complex flavor) instead of regular Green Beans then just steam them and add olive oil and black pepper. If you are using regular green beans then roast them.

Roasted Green Beans Recipe:

Preheat oven to 400°F.
For each serving:
1 cup green beans, stem ends cut off
1 tsp. olive oil
Black pepper to taste
1 tsp. fresh thyme, chopped

Place green beans in bowl. Add olive oil to coat green beans (if you use your hands it will coat more evenly). Add black pepper. Evenly distribute green beans in a single layer on a parchment lined baking pan. Bake at 400° F. for 8 to 10 minutes or until done, stirring once after 5 minutes. Sprinkle with thyme just before serving.

Day 9 Menu

Breakfast
Oatmeal with Dried Fruit and Nuts
½ Cherry Smoothie
Beverage of Choice

Snack anytime during the Day
Other ½ of Cherry Smoothie

Lunch
Tuna Arugula Pear Salad
Grapefruit
Beverage of Choice

Dinner
Quinoa Stuffed Portabella Mushroom
Tomato Salad with Parsley Dill Dressing
Chocolate Covered Strawberries
Beverage of Choice

Salt/Sodium for the Day: If you are limiting sodium to 1500 mg./day then you can add 1/8 tsp. salt to food or in cooking today beyond what is already in the recipes. If limiting to 2300 mg/day you can add an additional ½ tsp. salt to food or in cooking today.

Calories for the Day: If not restricting calories to 1600 per day you have the options of having extra Oatmeal at Breakfast, extra salad at Lunch and a second stuffed mushroom, more Salad and additional Chocolate covered Strawberries at Dinner.

Recipes

Breakfast: Oatmeal with Dried Fruit and Walnuts, ½ Cherry Smoothie.

Oatmeal recipe: Makes 1 serving.

¼ cup steel cut oats (may substitute rolled oats if you prefer)
1 cup unsweetened almond milk
1/4 tsp. ground cinnamon, or to taste
1/8 tsp. ground ginger, or to taste
1/2 tsp. vanilla, or to taste
1 Tbsp. raisins
4 dried apricots, chopped
1 tsp. honey or maple syrup
1 Tbsp. walnuts, chopped
1 Tbsp. flaxseed (optional, just adds 37 calories and has lots of
    health benefits)

Prepare oatmeal according to package directions using almond milk instead of water. Mix in cinnamon, ginger, vanilla, raisins, apricots, honey (or maple syrup), walnuts and flaxseed. Once cooked to desired consistency serve immediately.

Cherry Smoothie recipe: Makes 1 Smoothie.   Drink ½ at Breakfast and ½ as a snack.

Blend all of the following ingredients in a high-speed blender until smooth:
1 cup plain nonfat Greek Yogurt (containing 300 mg Calcium per
    cup serving. Nutrition label will say 30% of the RDA for Calcium)
½ cup frozen beets
½ cup frozen cherries
1 medium banana
1 Tbsp. flaxseed (optional, just adds 37 calories and has lots of
    health benefits)

Add additional water or ice cubes if a different consistency is desired.
If you have parsley or other greens that you need to use before they go bad then add them to your smoothie – don't let them go to waste.

Lunch: Tuna Arugula Pear Salad

Tuna Arugula Pear Salad Recipe
Per person:
1 cup Arugula
1 ripe Pear, cut in bite size pieces
12 purple grapes, cut in half
2 ounces low sodium tuna packed in water, drained
2 cups Bibb or Butterhead Lettuce (can substitute another type of
    lettuce or use more Arugula)
2 Tbsp. Feta Cheese
1 Tbsp. walnuts

Balsamic Dressing:
3 Tbsp. balsamic vinegar
3 Tbsp. honey
1 Tbsp. plain nonfat Greek yogurt
1 tsp. Dijon mustard
¼ cup walnut oil (may substitute olive oil)

Mix balsamic vinegar, honey, yogurt and mustard in a small bowl
and then gradually whisk in the oil. Or if you prefer mix all dressing
ingredients in a jar and shake until well blended.

In salad bowl mix arugula, pear, grapes, tuna and lettuce. Mix in 2
Tbsp. balsamic dressing per person. Top salad with Feta cheese
and walnuts.

Dinner: Quinoa Stuffed Portabella Mushroom, Tomato Salad,
Chocolate covered Strawberries.

Quinoa Stuffed Portabella Mushrooms Recipe: Makes 2
servings

Preheat oven to 375° F

¼ cup quinoa
¼ cup white wine (optional)
½ cup water
2 tsp. olive oil – divided in half
2 cloves garlic, minced
2 green onions, chopped
2 cups fresh spinach

1 cup fresh arugula
1/8 tsp. sea salt
2 Tbsp. pumpkin seeds
2 Tbsp. dried cranberries, preferably unsweetened which are a little
hard to find
2 large Portabella mushrooms, cleaned with stems removed (be
    sure to pick mushrooms that are a good size for stuffing)
2 Tbsp. Feta cheese

Rinse quinoa well. In small saucepan bring water and white wine to
a boil. Add quinoa and reduce heat to simmer. Cover pan and cook
until done, about 15 minutes.

Heat 1 tsp. olive oil in large skillet over medium heat. Sauté garlic
and green onions about 1 minute. Mix spinach and arugula into
garlic onion mixture, stirring until spinach and arugula leaves are
wilted, about 2 to 3 minutes. Mix in salt, pumpkin seeds and dried
cranberries. Transfer to bowl. Add quinoa to spinach arugula
mixture and set aside.

In skillet, heat 1 tsp. olive oil over medium heat. Cook Portabella
mushrooms cap side down for 2 minutes. Turn over and cook
another 2 minutes. Turn to cap side again and cook 2 minutes.
Turn over and cook another 2 minutes. Remove mushrooms from
pan and drain on paper towel.

Fill each Portobello mushroom with the quinoa mixture and top with
1 Tbsp. feta cheese each. Warm mushrooms in 375°F. oven for 5
minutes or until cheese melts.

Tomato Salad with Parsley Dill Dressing Recipe: 1 cup cherry
tomatoes cut in half or assorted sliced tomatoes per serving.

Parsley Dill Dressing: Makes 1 cup of Dressing

Put all of the following ingredients in a blender and blend until
smooth. Refrigerate.
¾ cup Plain nonfat Greek Yogurt
½ cup chopped Flat leaf Parsley
2 Tbsp. olive oil
2 Tbsp. lemon juice
2 Tbsp. fresh dill or 2 tsp. dried dill
1 tsp. maple syrup

1/8 tsp. kosher or sea salt

Top each serving of tomatoes with 2 Tbsp. Parsley Dill Dressing.

Chocolate Covered Strawberries Recipe: 4 medium to large strawberries and 2 squares 85% cocoa chocolate per person (if the 85% is too intense for you then you can use a lower cocoa content, which will have more sugar, but try not to go below 70% cocoa content). I like Lindt Chocolate Bars, which are available at many stores and on the Internet.

Wash strawberries and gently pat dry with paper towel. Place the chocolate in a microwave safe container. Set microwave on medium setting and microwave for 10 seconds, and then stir. Microwave another 10 seconds and stir again. Continue microwaving and stirring in 10 second intervals until melted completely. If you prefer you can melt the chocolate on low in a pan on the stove, stirring often or in a double boiler.
Dip whole strawberries in melted chocolate, holding strawberries by the stems. Place on wax paper and allow chocolate to solidify. The chocolate will solidify more quickly if you refrigerate the dipped strawberries. If you are not going to eat them right away then refrigerate. I think they are better at room temperature.

Day 10 Menu

Breakfast
Almond Molasses Muffins
Scrambled, Poached, Hard/Soft Boiled or Fried
Egg
½ Grapefruit
Beverage of Choice

Snack anytime during the day
Raspberry Smoothie

Lunch
Green Salad with Tuna
Beverage of Choice

Dinner
Red Lentil Sweet Potato Soup
Whole Grain Bread, Roll or Crackers
Apple or fruit of choice
Beverage of Choice

Salt/Sodium for the Day: If you are limiting sodium to 1500 mg./day then you should not add salt to food or in cooking today beyond what is already in the recipes. The artichokes in the Lunch salad are in a jar, not canned and have 90 mg sodium per serving. If limiting to 2300 mg/day you can add an additional 3/8 tsp. salt to food or in cooking today.

Calories for the Day: If not restricting calories to 1600 per day you have the options of adding almond butter to toasted muffins for Breakfast, having extra salad at Lunch and more Soup at Dinner.

Recipes
Breakfast: 2 Molasses muffins (Recipe Day 6), 1 Egg (or 2 egg whites) – cooked anyway you like, 1/2 Grapefruit. Just use 1 tsp. olive oil in preparing egg if limiting calories to 1600.

Snack anytime during the day: Raspberry Smoothie

Raspberry Smoothie recipe: Makes 1 Smoothie

Blend all of the following ingredients in a high-speed blender until smooth:
1 ¼ cup of unsweetened Almond Milk (Calcium calculation based on
     using almond milk containing 300 mg Calcium per 8 ounces or
     30% of the Calcium RDA. If using a product higher than 300
     then use only amount of Almond Milk required for 300 mg.
     Calcium and use water for the rest of the liquid).
1 cup raw kale
1/2 cup raspberries (may substitute another fruit)
1 medium banana
1 Tbsp. flaxseed (optional, just adds 37 calories and has lots of
     health benefits)

Add additional water or ice cubes if a different consistency is desired.
If you have parsley or other greens that you need to use before they go bad then add them to your smoothie – don't let them go to waste.

Lunch: Green Salad with Tuna.

Green Salad with Tuna recipe:

Mix the following ingredients per person:
3 small quartered and marinated artichoke hearts (in a jar not
     canned – 90 mg sodium)
1 cup Arugula
1 cup Romaine Lettuce, torn into bite size pieces
2 Tbsp. chopped celery
½ cup cherry tomatoes, cut in half
2 ounces canned low sodium tuna, drained
Add ¼ cup Parsley Dill dressing from yesterday (see Day 2 for recipe)

Dinner: Red Lentil Sweet Potato Soup, 1 serving Whole grain bread, roll or crackers, 1 Apple or fruit of choice.

Red Lentil Sweet Potato Soup recipe: Makes 6 servings. Make enough to have leftovers for Lunch Day 12.

Preheat oven to 400° F.

3 medium sweet potatoes, peeled and cut into bite size pieces
1 medium red bell pepper, cut into bite size pieces
1 Tbsp. olive oil and 1 tsp. olive oil, divided
¼ tsp. cayenne pepper
½ tsp. nutmeg, ground
1 tsp. sweet paprika
1 tsp. cinnamon, ground
2 yellow onions, chopped
4 garlic cloves, minced
8 cups low sodium vegetable broth
½ cup white wine (optional, can substitute water)
2 cups red lentils, rinsed
2 Bay leaves
½ tsp. allspice, ground
½ tsp. coriander, ground
½ tsp. cloves, ground
½ tsp. ginger, ground
¼ tsp. sea salt

Topping:
¾ cup Greek Yogurt
¼ cup cilantro, chopped
2 Tbsp. Lime Juice

2 Tbsp. pumpkin seeds
6 Lime wedges

In large bowl mix sweet potato and red bell pepper with 1 Tbsp. olive oil, cayenne pepper, nutmeg, paprika and cinnamon. Be sure to coat all pieces well. (I find it is easier to use my hands to mix it). Place vegetables in a single layer on a parchment lined baking sheet and roast for 30 minutes at 400°.

Heat 1 tsp. olive oil in large pot over medium heat. Add onions and garlic and sauté about 5 minutes. Mix vegetable broth, wine, lentils and bay leaves into onion mixture. Add roasted sweet potato and bell pepper. Mix allspice, coriander, cloves, ginger and salt into soup. Simmer soup until lentils are done, about 20 to 30 minutes.

For topping mix yogurt, cilantro and lime juice in a small bowl.

Remove bay leaves from soup. Serve in soup bowls. Top each serving with 2 Tbsp. yogurt topping and 1 tsp. pumpkin seeds. Serve with Lime wedges.

Day 11 Menu

Breakfast
Granola with Blueberries or Fruit of Choice
Beverage of Choice

Snack anytime during the day
Mango Smoothie

Lunch
Shrimp Sweet Potato Cocktail
Apple or Fruit of choice
Beverage of Choice

Dinner
Pasta with Spinach and Tomatoes
Whole Grain Roll or Bread
Orange with Dark Chocolate
Beverage of Choice

Salt/Sodium for the Day: If you are limiting sodium to 1500 mg./day then you should not add salt to food or in cooking today beyond what is already in the recipes. If limiting to 2300 mg/day you can add an additional 3/8 tsp. salt to food or in cooking today.

Calories for the Day: If not restricting calories to 1600 per day you have the options of having more Granola and fruit at Breakfast, an extra 2 ounces shrimp at Lunch and extra pasta, bread, orange and chocolate at Dinner.

Recipes

Breakfast: ½ cup Granola with ¾ cup Non-fat Plain Greek Yogurt, 1 cup blueberries and 1 tsp. honey or maple syrup if desired. May substitute unsweetened Almond Milk or a non-dairy yogurt for Greek Yogurt. May substitute another fruit for blueberries.
Use the Granola recipe from Day 2.

Snack Anytime during the day: Mango Smoothie
Mango Smoothie recipe:

Blend all of the following ingredients in a high-speed blender until smooth:

¾ cup of unsweetened Almond Milk (Calcium calculation based on using almond milk containing 300 mg Calcium per 8 ounces or 30% of the Calcium RDA. If using a product higher than 300 mg. then use only amount of Almond Milk required for 300 mg. Calcium and use water for the rest of the liquid).

¼ cup plain nonfat Greek Yogurt (containing 300 mg Calcium per 1 cup serving. Nutrition label will say 30% of the RDA for Calcium)

1 cup raw kale

1/2 cup frozen or fresh mango (may substitute another fruit for mango)

1 medium banana

1 Tbsp. flaxseed (optional, just adds 37 calories and has lots of health benefits)

Add additional water or ice cubes if a different consistency is desired.
If you have parsley or other greens that you need to use before they go bad then add them to your smoothie – don't let them go to waste.

Lunch: Shrimp Sweet Potato Cocktail, 1 Apple.

Shrimp Sweet Potato Cocktail Recipe: Makes 2 servings

Preheat oven to 400° F.

1 Sweet Potato, cut into bite size pieces
1 cup Pineapple chunks, fresh or canned in juice
½ cup cherry Tomatoes
1 Tbsp. Balsamic vinegar (pineapple or regular)
1 tsp. olive oil
1/8 tsp. cayenne pepper

6 ounces cooked Shrimp
2 Tbsp. Cilantro, chopped
1 jalapeno pepper, finely chopped
2 Lime wedges
Mix sweet potato. pineapple, tomatoes, balsamic vinegar, olive oil and cayenne pepper so that vegetables are well coated in vinegar, oil and pepper.   Evenly distribute sweet potato, pineapple and tomato mixture on a parchment lined baking sheet. Roast at 400° F. for 20 to 25 minutes or until tomatoes pop and sweet potato is tender.

Allow vegetable mixture to cool slightly then add shrimp, cilantro and jalapeno. Serve with lime wedges.

Dinner: Whole Wheat Pasta with Spinach and Tomatoes, Whole Grain Roll or Bread (Garlic Bread if you like), 1 Orange with 2 squares Dark Chocolate (preferably 85% Cocoa content).

Whole Grain Pasta with Spinach and Tomatoes Recipe

Per Person:
1 tsp. olive oil
1 garlic clove, finely chopped
4 cups fresh raw spinach
2/3 cup dry whole wheat penne or other whole grain pasta, cooked
1 cup cherry tomatoes, cut in half
1/8 tsp. sea salt
2 Tbsp. good quality Parmesan cheese

Heat olive oil in large pot or skillet. Add garlic and spinach (it is ok if the spinach still has water clinging to it from washing) and cook until spinach wilts, stirring frequently.   Add cooked pasta, cherry tomatoes and salt to spinach mixture. Remove and serve once pasta is thoroughly heated. Top with Parmesan cheese. If you can afford some extra calories you can drizzle a little high quality olive oil over the top before serving.

Day 12 Menu

Breakfast
Almond Toast
Orange sections or fruit of choice
1/2 Peach Smoothie
Beverage of Choice

Snack Anytime during the Day
Other 1/2 of Peach Smoothie

Lunch
Red Lentil Sweet Potato Soup
Kiwi or fruit of Choice
Beverage of Choice

Dinner
Fish Tacos
Avocado
Apple or Fruit of Choice
Beverage of Choice

Salt/Sodium for the Day: If you are limiting sodium to 1500 mg./day then you can add 1/8 tsp. salt to food or in cooking today beyond what is already in the recipes. If limiting to 2300 mg/day you can add an additional ½ tsp. salt to food or in cooking today.

Calories for the Day: If not restricting calories to 1600 per day you have the options of having more soup and fruit and you can add a piece of whole grain bread at Lunch and you can eat more avocado and fruit at Dinner.

Recipes:

Breakfast: Almond Toast, 1 orange or fruit of choice and ½ of Peach Smoothie.

Spread 2 Tbsp. almond butter on 1 slice toasted whole grain bread. Prepare Peach Smoothie. May substitute another fruit for Peaches.

Peach Smoothie recipe: To be divided to drink ½ at breakfast and ½ as a snack anytime during the day.

Blend all of the following ingredients in a high-speed blender until smooth:

1 ½ cup of unsweetened Almond Milk (Calcium calculation based on using almond milk containing 300 mg Calcium per 8 ounces or 30% of the Calcium RDA. If using a product higher than 300 mg. then use only amount of Almond Milk required for 300 mg. Calcium and use water for the rest of the liquid).

1/2 cup plain nonfat Greek Yogurt (containing 300 mg Calcium per 1 cup serving. Nutrition label will say 30% of the RDA for Calcium)

1 cup raw kale

1 cup raw spinach

1 cup frozen or fresh peaches (may substitute another fruit for peaches)

1 medium banana

1 Tbsp. flaxseed (optional, just adds 37 calories and has lots of health benefits)

Add additional water or ice cubes if a different consistency is desired.

If you have parsley or other greens that you need to use before they go bad then add them to your smoothie – don't let them go to waste.

Lunch: Red Lentil Soup (Leftover from Day 10), Kiwi or fruit of choice.

Dinner: Fish Tacos, ½ avocado, Apple or fruit of choice.

Fish Taco Recipe: Serves 4 – half recipe for 2

Sauce:
1 cup plain nonfat Greek Yogurt
1/8 tsp. cayenne pepper

1 tsp. fresh lime juice
1/8 tsp. cumin, ground
2 Tbsp. Cilantro, chopped
¼ tsp. sea salt
2 tsp. honey
1/8 tsp. chili powder, more if you like a spicier, hotter sauce

For sauce: In small bowl mix yogurt, cayenne pepper, lime juice, cumin, cilantro, salt, honey and chili powder.

Pico de Gallo:
2 Tbsp. Cilantro, chopped
2 Tbsp. chopped onion
1 Jalapeno, chopped finely
½ cup chopped tomato
1 clove garlic, minced

For Pico de Gallo: In small bowl mix cilantro, onion, jalapeno, tomato and garlic.

Fish:
1 pound fish, cut into ½" pieces
¼ cup Cilantro, chopped
¼ tsp. sea salt
1/4 tsp. cumin, ground
1/4 tsp. chili powder
2 tsp. olive oil

In a medium bowl mix fish, cilantro, salt, cumin and chili powder together. Heat olive oil over medium heat in large skillet. Cook fish until done, about 3 to 5 minutes.

8 corn tortillas – warmed
2 cups shredded cabbage
4 lime wedges

Serve fish in warmed corn tortillas with sauce, pico de gallo and shredded cabbage. Serve with lime wedge on the side. Allow ½ avocado per person to be used as avocado chunks in tacos or as side of guacamole.

Day 13 Menu

Breakfast
Apricot Date Muffins
Scrambled, Poached, Hard/Soft Boiled or Fried Egg
Beverage of Choice

Lunch
Hummus
Broccoli & Cauliflower
Whole Grain Crackers or Bread
½ Grapefruit
Beverage of Choice

Dinner
Spinach Tomato Pizza
Mixed Greens Salad with Parsley Dill Dressing
Beverage of Choice

Salt/Sodium for the Day: If you are limiting sodium to 1500 mg./day then you should not add salt to food or in cooking today beyond what is already in the recipes and you should omit the salt in the Pizza topping. If limiting to 2300 mg/day you can add an additional ¼ tsp. salt to food or in cooking today.

Calories for the Day: If not restricting calories to 1600 per day you have the options of having extra muffins at Breakfast, extra hummus at Lunch and more Pizza and Salad with dressing at Dinner.

Recipes:

Breakfast: 2 Apricot muffins, 1 Egg – scrambled, fried, hard or soft boiled or poached.

Apricot Date Muffins Recipe: Makes 12 muffins. Make enough to freeze for Breakfast on Day 16.

Preheat oven to 400° F.

1 cup almond meal
½ cup teff flour
½ cup garbanzo bean flour
2 tsp. baking powder
½ tsp. ground cinnamon and additional to sprinkle on top of muffins
    if desired
½ tsp. ground anise seed
¼ tsp. salt
½ cup chopped dried dates (about 8 to 10 dates)
½ cup chopped dried apricots, preferably unsulphured
2 eggs
¼ cup plus 2 Tbsp. maple syrup
1/3 cup almond butter
½ cup orange juice – from concentrate with Calcium added
1 Tbsp. orange zest (preferably from an organic orange)
Anise seeds for tops of muffins (optional)

Preheat oven to 400°. Prepare 12-cup muffin pan.

In medium bowl mix almond meal, teff flour, garbanzo bean flour, baking powder, cinnamon, anise, and salt. Add dates and apricots combining so that fruits are evenly distributed and well coated with dry flour mixture. In medium bowl mix eggs, maple syrup, almond butter, orange juice and orange zest until smooth. Add liquid mixture to flour mixture and mix well.

Divide batter up into 12 muffin tins. Muffin tins will be filled to the top. If desired, sprinkle tops of muffins with additional cinnamon and anise seeds (or ground anise).

Bake at 400° for 15 to 20 minutes or until toothpick inserted in center of muffins comes out clean and tops spring back when lightly touched. If baking in paper muffin cups remove from pan immediately and cool on wire cooling rack. If not using paper muffin cups let cool 5 minutes in pan and then remove muffins and put on wire cooling rack. Freeze leftovers for Day 16.

Teff Flour, Almond Meal and Garbanzo bean flour can be purchased at Trader Jo's, Whole Foods and Central Market and some grocery stores carry the specialty flours as well. If you do not have access to a store carrying these products you can order them on line and one source is Bob's Red Mill at www.bobsredmill.com

Lunch: 1/2 cup Hummus with raw Broccoli (as much as you want) and raw Cauliflower (as much as you want) plus 6 whole grain crackers or a slice of whole grain bread (I like Flackers – crackers made from flax seeds or try Multi Grain Wasa Flatbreads) per person, ½ Grapefruit.

Dinner: 2 slices Spinach Tomato Pizza, 2 cups or more mixed greens with some grated carrot as a salad with 2 Tbsp. Parsley Dill Dressing (recipe Day 2).

Spinach Tomato Pizza Recipe: Divide into 6 slices per Pizza. Make enough to have 1 slice for Lunch tomorrow.

Preheat oven to 500°F. If you use a pizza stone Cook's Illustrated recommends preheating the stone for an hour at 500°F before baking Pizza on the stone.   Cook's test kitchen found 30 to 45 minutes was not enough and that an hour produces the best crisp well browned crust.   Cook's also recommends using an inverted baking sheet if you don't have a pizza stone and you only need to preheat it for 30 minutes since it has less mass than a stone.

If you prefer you can substitute a good whole grain pre-made Pizza dough rather than making your own.   Check out Brooklyn 100% Whole Wheat Pizza Dough in the Frozen food section of your grocery store. Pillsbury Artisan Pizza Crust with whole grain in the refrigerator section of the grocery store and IL Fornaio Wheat Pizza Dough in the Frozen food section aren't 100% whole grain options but do contain some whole wheat flour.

Pizza Crust – makes two 12" Pizza crust:
(Freeze one crust or finished pizza for another meal if you only need one for this meal)

1 envelope dry yeast
1 cup plus 3 Tbsp. warm water (105°F to 115°F)
1 tsp. honey
1¼ cups bread flour (for a 100% whole grain crust use all whole
    wheat flour)
1¼ cups whole wheat flour
1 Tbsp. olive oil
¾ tsp. sea salt

In small bowl sprinkle yeast over warm water. Stir in honey. Let stand until foamy.

You can mix the ingredients by hand but a food processor works better. In food processor work bowl using steel knife attachment combine bread flour, whole wheat flour, oil and salt. With machine running add yeast mixture through feed tube and process 30 seconds. If dough sticks to bowl add more bread flour through feed tube 1 Tbsp. at a time, allowing flour to incorporate before adding additional flour, if needed. If dough is dry add water through feed tube 1 tsp. at a time, allowing water to incorporate into dough before adding additional water. Process dough until smooth and elastic, about 1 minute.
Transfer dough to large oiled bowl, turning to coat entire dough surface. Cover bowl with plastic wrap and lint free towel. Let dough rise in warm place until doubled in volume, about 1 hour. It also works well to make the dough one or 2 days ahead and refrigerate it rather than allowing it to rise at room temperature.

Punch down dough. Oil bottom of pizza pans with olive oil or use a pizza stone. Roll out dough in circles and fit to pizza pan or slide on to Pizza stone. If you have chosen to refrigerate the dough instead of allowing it to rise at room temperature then remove from refrigerator when ready to use, roll and fit in to pizza pans or on to stone.

Sauce for 1 Pizza – double for 2:
If you are in a hurry you can substitute canned tomato sauce or pasta sauce, preferably a
    low salt version.
Or you can make your own Sauce:

In a food processor bowl process until smooth and refrigerate until ready to use:
3 garlic cloves, minced
1 (28 ounce) can whole peeled tomatoes, preferably low salt,
    drained
1 Tbsp. fresh oregano, chopped or 1 tsp. dried oregano
1 tsp. red wine or red wine vinegar

Topping for 1 Pizza – double for 2:
1 tsp. Olive oil for sautéing spinach and small amount of olive oil for brushing top of
    tomatoes
1 pound fresh Spinach
¼ tsp. sea salt (if you want to limit sodium to 1500 mg/day leave this
    out)
¼ tsp. red pepper
¼ tsp. nutmeg, ground
3 ounces part skim mozzarella cheese, grated
2 medium tomatoes, sliced (can use cherry tomatoes but don't slice
    – just let them split or pop while cooking)

Heat 1 tsp. olive oil in large pot. Add Spinach (it works well to let any water left from rinsing spinach, if not using prewashed spinach, still cling to leaves) and stir regularly until just wilted. Add salt, pepper and nutmeg. Remove from pot and drain on paper or lint free cloth towel.

To assemble Pizza spread tomato sauce over Pizza leaving a ½ inch border around the edge. Top with ½ of the cheese. Layer Spinach over top of cheese. Place tomato slices on top of cheese, spreading evenly around Pizza. Lightly brush tomato slices with olive oil (if using cherry tomatoes mix them in a bowl with oil prior to putting on Pizza). Top with remaining cheese. Be sure crust forms a border around toppings.

Bake at 500°F until crust is well browned and cheese is bubbly and beginning to brown, about 10 minutes. Rotate pizza half way through cooking time. Let pizza cool 5 minutes before cutting and serving. Slice each Pizza into 6 slices.

Day 14 Menu

Breakfast
Potato and Egg Taco
Orange and Kiwi Salad
½ Cherry Smoothie
Beverage of Choice

Snack anytime during the day
Other 1/2 of Cherry Smoothie

Lunch
Spinach Tomato Pizza
Mixed Greens Salad with Parsley Dill Dressing
Beverage of Choice

Dinner
Roast Chicken
Green Beans
Sweet Potato
Blueberry "Not Really Ice Cream"
Beverage of Choice

Salt/Sodium for the Day: If you are limiting sodium to 1500 mg./day then you need to purchase low sodium tortillas for Breakfast Taco and should not add salt to food or in cooking today beyond what is already in the recipes. If limiting to 2300 mg/day you can add an additional ¼ tsp. salt to food or in cooking today and do not have to use low salt tortillas.

Calories for the Day: If not restricting calories to 1600 per day you have the options of having a second Breakfast Taco at Breakfast, extra Pizza and salad at Lunch and 2 ounces additional chicken, extra vegetables and extra Blueberry "Not Really Ice Cream" at Dinner.

Recipes:
Breakfast: 1 Potato and Egg taco, Orange Kiwi Salad, ½ Cherry Smoothie

Recipe for Breakfast Taco:
For each person, in a skillet scramble 1 egg (or 2 egg whites) in 1 tsp. olive oil, add ½ cup warm cooked potato, cut in chunks. Serve in a warm whole grain tortilla with hot sauce.

Serve with fruit salad of ½ orange, divided into sections and ½ kiwi, sliced into bite size pieces per person.

Cherry Smoothie recipe: To be divided to drink ½ at breakfast and ½ as snack.

Blend all of the following ingredients in a high-speed blender until smooth:
1 ¼ cup of unsweetened Almond Milk (Calcium calculation based on using almond milk containing 300 mg Calcium per 8 ounces or 30% of the Calcium RDA. If using a product higher than 300 mg. then use only amount of Almond Milk required for 300 mg. Calcium and use water for the rest of the liquid).
1/4 cup plain nonfat Greek Yogurt (containing 300 mg Calcium per 1 cup serving. Nutrition label will say 30% of the RDA for Calcium)
1 cup frozen beets
1 cup frozen cherries
1 medium banana
1 Tbsp. flaxseed (optional, just adds 37 calories and has lots of health benefits)

Add additional water or ice cubes if a different consistency is desired.
If you have parsley or other greens that you need to use before they go bad then add them to your smoothie – don't let them go to waste.

Lunch: 1 slice Spinach Tomato Pizza (leftover from yesterday) Mixed Greens Salad and grated carrots with Parsley Dill Dressing (same as yesterday dinner).

Dinner: Roast Chicken, Green Beans, Baked Sweet Potato and Blueberry "Not Really Ice Cream".

Roast Chicken Recipe: You can purchase already prepared Roasted or Rotisserie Chicken but try to purchase one that has not had a lot of salt and butter added to it.   Be sure you make or purchase enough to have leftover chicken for the Tarragon Chicken Salad for lunch for 2 days, tomorrow and Day 17.

3 ½ to 4 pound chicken, preferably organic free range
1 tsp. sea salt
¼ tsp. black pepper, ground
8 cloves garlic, 4 thinly sliced and 4 whole
5 sprigs rosemary or 1 Tbsp. dried, and extra for cavity, if desired
1 organic lemon cut in fourths
Olive oil

Season the chicken as soon as possible before cooking. You can season it the day before cooking or if you purchase the chicken the day of roasting season it as soon as you bring it home. To season remove the giblets from the cavity of the chicken. Mix salt and pepper and sprinkle all over chicken both inside and outside. Push garlic slices and rosemary under skin of chicken over breast and thighs. Put lemon and whole garlic in cavity of chicken. If desired add some extra rosemary sprigs to cavity of chicken. Tuck in wings.

When ready to roast preheat oven to 400°. Use olive oil to lightly oil roasting pan that is about the same size as the chicken.   Place chicken in pan breast side up and roast for 20 minutes.   Turn chicken breast side down and roast for another 20 minutes.   Turn chicken breast side up again and roast until done, about another 20 minutes. To test for doneness and be sure the meat is no longer red cut into the bird near the joint between the drumstick and thigh. Do not overcook which dries chicken out.

Let chicken rest for 10 minutes before serving.

If you can find haricots verts (French Green beans that are thinner, more tender with a more complex flavor), or fresh out of the garden Green Beans, instead of regular grocery store bought Green Beans then just steam them and add olive oil and black pepper. If you are using regular grocery store green beans then roast them.

Roasted Green Beans Recipe:

Preheat oven to 400°F.
For each serving:
1 cup green beans, stem ends cut off
1 tsp. olive oil
Black pepper to taste
1 tsp. fresh thyme, chopped (or ½ tsp. dried thyme)

Place green beans in bowl. Add olive oil to coat green beans (if you use your hands it will coat more evenly). Add black pepper. Evenly distribute green beans in a single layer on a parchment lined baking pan. Bake at 400° F. for 8 to 10 minutes or until done, stirring once after 5 minutes. Sprinkle with thyme just before serving.

Baked Sweet Potato Recipe: 1 potato per person. Scrub well and bake at 425° F. for 1 hour or until done. Pierce with fork after sweet potato has been in the oven for 30 minutes. If you have more than 1 tsp. of butter on the potato you will exceed 1600 calories for the day. I don't advocate the use of butter on a regular basis but there are certain foods that warrant butter and in my opinion a baked sweet potato is one of them.

Blueberry "Not Really Ice Cream" Recipe:

For each serving combine 1 cup frozen blueberries, ¼ cup nonfat plain Greek yogurt and 2 tsp. maple syrup in a food processor or blender. Blend until smooth. Serve immediately or put it in the freezer for a few minutes if you want a firmer consistency.

Day 15 Menu

Breakfast
Oatmeal with Walnuts and Banana
½ Strawberry Smoothie
Beverage of Choice

Lunch
Tarragon Chicken Salad with Avocado & Spinach
Beverage of Choice

Dinner
Lentil Burger
Sweet Potato Fries
Other 1/2 of Strawberry Smoothie
Beverage of Choice

Salt/Sodium for the Day: If you are limiting sodium to 1500 mg./day then you can add 1/8 tsp. salt to food or in cooking today beyond what is already in the recipes. If limiting to 2300 mg/day you can add an additional ½ tsp. salt to food or in cooking today.

Calories for the Day: If not restricting calories to 1600 per day you have the options of having additional avocado at Lunch, extra Sweet Potato Fries at Dinner and mayonnaise on your burger.

Recipes
Breakfast: Steel Cut Oatmeal with Walnuts and Banana, ½ of Strawberry Smoothie

Oatmeal recipe: Makes 1 serving.

¼ cup steel cut oats (may substitute rolled oats if you prefer)
1 cup unsweetened almond milk
1/4 tsp. ground cinnamon, or to taste
1/8 tsp. ground ginger, or to taste
1/2 tsp. vanilla, or to taste
1 tsp. honey or maple syrup
1 banana, sliced into bite size slices
1 Tbsp. walnuts, chopped
1 Tbsp. flaxseed (optional, just adds 37 calories and has lots of
    health benefits)

Prepare oatmeal according to package directions using almond milk instead of water. Mix in cinnamon, ginger, vanilla, honey (or maple syrup), banana, walnuts and flaxseed. Once cooked to desired consistency serve immediately.

Strawberry Smoothie recipe: To be divided to drink ½ at Breakfast and ½ at Dinner.

Blend all of the following ingredients in a high-speed blender until smooth:
¾ cup of unsweetened Almond Milk (Calcium calculation based on
    using almond milk containing 300 mg Calcium per 8 ounces or
    30% of the Calcium RDA. If using a product higher than 300 mg.
    then use only amount of Almond Milk required for 300 mg.
    Calcium and use water for the rest of the liquid).
¾ cup plain nonfat Greek Yogurt (containing 300 mg Calcium per 1
    cup serving. Nutrition label will say 30% of the RDA for Calcium)
1 cup raw kale
1 cup frozen or fresh strawberries (may substitute another fruit)
1 medium banana
1 Tbsp. flaxseed (optional, just adds 37 calories and has lots of
    health benefits.
Add additional water or ice cubes if a different consistency is desired.

If you have parsley or other greens that you need to use before they go bad then add them to your smoothie – don't let them go to waste.

Lunch: Tarragon Chicken Salad with Avocado.

Tarragon Chicken Salad Recipe: Makes 4 servings.   Make enough for Day 17 Lunch as well.

2 cups chopped cooked chicken
1 cup red grapes, halved
¼ cup chopped walnuts
1/3 cup dried cherries
¼ cup plain nonfat Greek yogurt
¼ cup canola mayonnaise (or olive oil mayo)
1 tsp. Dijon mustard
1/8 tsp. kosher or sea salt
½ tsp. dried tarragon or 1 tsp. fresh, chopped (can substitute
    Mexican Mint Marigold)
4 cups raw spinach
1 Avocado

Combine chicken, grapes, walnuts and cherries in medium bowl.

Combine yogurt, mayonnaise, mustard, salt and tarragon in small bowl.   Add yogurt mixture to chicken mixture. Mix well.   Cover and chill until ready to serve. Serve Chicken salad on bed of Spinach (at least 1 cup) with ¼ of an avocado, sliced and seasoned with lemon juice and black pepper (may have more avocado if not limiting calories to 1600).

Dinner: 1 Lentil Burger, Sweet Potato Fries, 2nd half of Strawberry Smoothie.

Lentil Burger Recipe: Makes 6 burgers

¼ cup brown rice
½ cup water
¾ tsp. curry powder – divided into ¼ tsp. and ½ tsp.
1 cup potato (cut in 2 inch chunks)
2 garlic cloves
½ cup red lentils
1 cup water
4 tsp. olive oil – divided in half

¼ yellow onion, chopped
1 medium carrot, chopped
¼ cup red bell pepper, chopped
¼ cup yellow bell pepper, chopped
2 large mushrooms, chopped
Black pepper to taste
2 Tbsp. chopped parsley
¼ tsp. kosher or sea salt
Mango Chutney or any type (make your own or buy one that has
    fruit as first ingredient & no or low sodium)
Fresh Spinach, at least 8 leaves per burger
6 whole grain hamburger buns

Cook brown rice according to package directions in ½ cup water with ¼ tsp. curry powder. Set aside.

In medium saucepan cover potatoes and garlic with water. Bring to a boil over high heat and reduce heat to medium and cook until done, 20 to 25 minutes. Drain well and mash mixture. Set aside.

In medium saucepan bring lentils and 1 cup water to a boil over high heat. Reduce heat to low, cover, and cook until lentils are consistency of a thick paste. Set aside.

In medium skillet heat 2 tsp. olive oil over medium heat. Add onion and sauté for 1 minute. Add carrots and bell peppers. Cook, stirring frequently for 5 minutes. Add mushrooms and cook until tender. Add black pepper to taste.

In large bowl mix rice, potato garlic mixture, lentils, vegetables, ½ tsp. curry powder, parsley and salt together until well blended.

Divide and shape mixture into 3-inch diameter, 1-inch thick patties. Patties are easier to handle if refrigerated at least one hour prior to cooking. Patties are also easier to flip if you don't make them any larger than 3-inch diameter.

In large skillet heat 2 tsp. olive oil over medium heat. Add patties and cook until brown on both sides, about 3 minutes per side.

Serve on whole grain buns with canola mayonnaise if not restricting calories to 1600, raw spinach (at least 8 leaves per burger) and mango chutney (1 Tbsp. if restricting calories to 1600/day). Can

Recipes:

Breakfast: Apricot muffins − 1 if limiting to 1600 calories (recipe from Day 13), and ½ of Mango Smoothie.

Mango Smoothie recipe: To be divided to drink ½ at breakfast and ½ at lunch.

Blend all of the following ingredients in a high-speed blender until smooth:

1 cup plain nonfat Greek Yogurt (containing 300 mg Calcium per 1 cup serving. Nutrition label will say 30% of the RDA for Calcium)
½ cup fresh or frozen mango (may substitute another fruit)
1 cup kale
1 medium banana
1 Tbsp. flaxseed (optional, just adds 37 calories and has lots of health benefits)

Add additional water or ice cubes if a different consistency is desired.

If you have parsley or other greens that you need to use before they go bad then add them to your smoothie − don't let them go to waste.

Lunch: Barley Cranberry Salad, remaining ½ of Mango Smoothie.

Barley Cranberry Salad Recipe: Makes 4 servings. Make enough for lunch on Day 19, too.

4 cups water
1 cup hulled or pearled barley, rinsed
1 15 oz. can No salt added Garbanzo Beans or 1 ¾ cups cooked garbanzo beans, drained. I like Eden No Salt Added canned beans with BPA free lining or try Whole Foods 365 Organic No salt added beans that are packed in cartons. If you have time cook your own from dried beans.
¼ cup dried cranberries, preferably unsweetened
¼ cup sunflower seeds
2 Tbsp. red onion, minced
¼ cup celery, chopped
¼ cup Italian flat leaf parsley, chopped
¼ tsp. sea salt
¼ cup olive oil
2 Tbsp. balsamic vinegar

2 tsp. lemon juice
8 cups spinach

Bring water to a boil in saucepan. Add barley, reduce heat, cover and cook for one hour. Cool.

In large bowl combine cooked barley, well drained Garbanzo beans, dried cranberries, sunflower seeds, onion, celery, parsley and salt.

In a jar mix olive oil, balsamic vinegar and lemon juice and shake will. Add to salad. Serve on bed of spinach, 2 cups spinach per serving.

Dinner: Pasta with Arugula and Mushrooms.

Whole Grain Pasta with Arugula and Mushrooms Recipe:

Per Person:
1 tsp. olive oil
1 garlic clove, finely chopped
¼ cup red bell pepper, chopped
1 cup sliced mushrooms
¼ cup white wine (may substitute water)
2 cups arugula
1 cup cherry tomatoes, cut in half (or you can roast these whole and use roasted)
¾ cup Navy beans (I like Eden No Salt Added canned beans with BPA free lining or try Whole Foods 365 Organic No salt added beans that are packed in cartons. If you have time cook your own from dried beans).
1/4 tsp. sea salt
2 Tbsp. flat leaf parsley, chopped
2/3 cup dry whole wheat penne or other whole grain pasta cooked according to package directions and drained
2 Tbsp. Parmesan cheese – divided in half
1 Tbsp. pine nuts, toasted
Fresh lemon juice to taste

Heat olive oil in large skillet. Add garlic, red bell pepper and mushrooms. Stirring frequently, cook for 1 minute. Add white wine or water to skillet. Cook until red bell pepper and mushrooms are tender, stirring frequently. Add arugula, cherry tomatoes, navy beans and salt to skillet. Once arugula is just wilted add parsley.

Stir 1 Tbsp. Parmesan cheese into cooked, warm pasta. Serve vegetables over pasta. Top with remaining 1 Tbsp. Parmesan cheese and pine nuts. Serve with lemon wedges and add lemon juice to taste.

If you can afford the extra calories drizzle a little high quality olive oil over the pasta.

Day 17 Menu

Breakfast
Granola with Blueberries
Beverage of Choice

Snack anytime during the Day
Peach Smoothie

Lunch
Tarragon Chicken Salad with Avocado and Spinach
Beverage of Choice

Dinner
Quinoa Stuffed Acorn Squash
Whole Grain Bread or Roll
Berries Romanoff
Beverage of Choice

Salt/Sodium for the Day: If you are limiting sodium to 1500 mg./day then you may add 1/8 tsp. salt to food or in cooking today beyond what is already in the recipes. If limiting to 2300 mg/day you can add an additional ½ tsp. salt to food or in cooking today.

Calories for the Day: If not restricting calories to 1600 per day you have the options of having more Granola and fruit at Breakfast, more chicken salad and avocado at Lunch and a second stuffed Acorn Squash and a larger portion of Berries Romanoff at Dinner.

Recipes

Breakfast: ½ cup Granola with ¾ cup Non-fat Plain Greek Yogurt, 1 cup blueberries and 1 tsp. honey or maple syrup if desired. May substitute unsweetened Almond Milk or a non-dairy yogurt for Greek Yogurt. May substitute another fruit or combination of fruit for blueberries. Use the Granola recipe from Day 2.

Snack Anytime during the day: Peach Smoothie
Peach Smoothie recipe:

Blend all of the following ingredients in a high-speed blender until smooth:

1 ¼ cup of unsweetened Almond Milk (Calcium calculation based on using almond milk containing 300 mg Calcium per 8 ounces or 30% of the Calcium RDA. If using a product higher than 300 mg. then use only amount of Almond Milk required for 300 mg. Calcium and use water for the rest of the liquid).

1 cup raw kale

1/2 cup frozen or fresh peaches (may substitute another fruit for peaches)

1 medium banana

1 Tbsp. flaxseed (optional, just adds 37 calories and has lots of health benefits)

Add additional water or ice cubes if a different consistency is desired.

If you have parsley or other greens that you need to use before they go bad then add them to your smoothie – don't let them go to waste.

Lunch: Tarragon Chicken Salad Leftover from Day 15.

Dinner: Quinoa Stuffed Acorn Squash, Slice of whole grain bread or 1 whole grain roll, Berries Romanoff.

Quinoa stuffed Acorn Squash Recipe: Makes 2 servings

Preheat oven to 400° F.

1 Acorn squash
¼ tsp. olive oil
¼ cup Orange juice
1/8 tsp. turmeric
Pinch of saffron threads, crushed (this is an expensive spice but a
    little goes a long way and it adds great flavor but you can leave
    this out and it will still be good – add a little more turmeric if you
    don't use the saffron)
3/4 cup water
½ cup Quinoa, rinsed
2 Tbsp. sliced almonds, toasted
2 Tbsp. dried apricots (preferably unsulphured), chopped
2 Tbsp. raisins
¼ tsp. sea salt
Juice of 1 lemon

Slice Acorn Squash in half and remove seeds. Brush inside with
olive oil. Bake, cut side up, at 400° F. until tender, about 30 to 40
minutes. Remove from oven and reduce heat to 350° F.

In a medium saucepan, bring orange juice, turmeric, saffron and
water to a boil. Add quinoa, cover and reduce heat to low. Simmer
quinoa until liquid is absorbed and quinoa is done.

Stir almonds, apricots, raisins, salt and lemon juice into quinoa.

Stuff acorn squash with quinoa mixture and heat at 350° for 15
minutes or until warm.

Recipe for Berries Romanoff:

For each serving carefully mix ¼ cup fresh raspberries, ¼ cup fresh
blackberries, ¼ cup fresh blueberries and ¼ cup fresh strawberries
per person. You can use whatever combination you want of berries
if you don't want to use 4 kinds. Top with ½ cup plain nonfat Greek
yogurt mixed with 1 tsp. maple syrup, 1 tsp. orange liquor such as
Grand Marnier or Cointreau (may substitute orange juice) and 1 tsp.
brandy or brandy extract (may substitute vanilla).

Day 18 Menu

Breakfast
Almond Toast
½ of Blueberry Smoothie
Beverage of Choice

Lunch
Grapefruit and Greens Salad
Whole Grain Bread or Roll
Other 1/2 of Blueberry Smoothie
Beverage of Choice

Dinner
Filet Mignon
Swiss Chard
Baked Potato
Whole Grain Bread or Roll
Beverage of Choice

Salt/Sodium for the Day: If you are limiting sodium to 1500 mg./day do not add additional salt to food or in cooking today beyond what is already in the recipes and use unsalted butter at dinner. If limiting to 2300 mg/day you can add an additional 3/8 tsp. salt to food or in cooking today.

Calories for the Day: If not restricting calories to 1600 per day you have the options of having more salad and salad dressing at Lunch and an additional 2 ounces of filet mignon at Dinner.

Recipes:
Breakfast: Almond Toast, ½ of Blueberry Smoothie.

Spread 2 Tbsp. almond butter on 1 slice toasted whole grain bread. Prepare Blueberry Smoothie.   May substitute another fruit for Blueberries.

Blueberry Smoothie recipe: To be divided to drink ½ at breakfast and ½ as lunch.

Blend all of the following ingredients in a high-speed blender until smooth:

3/4 cup of unsweetened Almond Milk (Calcium calculation based on using almond milk containing 300 mg Calcium per 8 ounces or 30% of the Calcium RDA. If using a product higher than 300 mg. then use only amount of Almond Milk required for 300 mg. Calcium and use water for the rest of the liquid).

3/4 cup plain nonfat Greek Yogurt (containing 300 mg Calcium per 1 cup serving. Nutrition label will say 30% of the RDA for Calcium)

2 cups raw kale

1 cup frozen or fresh blueberries (may substitute another fruit for blueberries)

1 medium banana

1 Tbsp. flaxseed (optional, just adds 37 calories and has lots of health benefits)

Add additional water or ice cubes if a different consistency is desired.

If you have parsley or other greens that you need to use before they go bad then add them to your smoothie – don't let them go to waste.

Lunch: Grapefruit and Greens Salad, Whole grain roll or bread, 2nd half of Blueberry Smoothie.

Grapefruit and Greens Salad Recipe:

Per Person:

2 cups red lettuce, or any combination of lettuce

½ grapefruit, separated into sections

1 Tbsp. sunflower seeds

2 Tbsp. blue cheese (you can substitute 1 ounce of another type cheese like Feta)

2 Tbsp. Lemon maple dressing

To make dressing put the following ingredients in a jar and shake well (easy way) or mix maple syrup, lemon juice and Dijon mustard in small bowl. Gradually whisk in olive oil until well mixed (the proper way):

2 Tbsp. 100% Maple syrup
¼ cup lemon juice
1 Tbsp. Dijon Mustard
¼ cup olive oil

To assemble salad toss greens with Lemon Maple dressing. Top salad with grapefruit sections, sunflower seeds and blue cheese.

Dinner: Filet Mignon, Baked Potato, Swiss Chard, Whole grain bread or roll.

Per Person:
Prepare 4 ounce Filet Mignon according to preferred cooking method and doneness.

Bake potato at 425°F for 1 hour or until done. Pierce with fork 30 minutes into cooking time. Do not wrap in foil to cook. If restricting calories to 1600 limit butter for potato to 2 tsp. (In my opinion an occasional splurge of butter is OK).

In skillet over medium heat sauté 3 cups Swiss chard in 1 tsp. olive oil until tender. Add black pepper to taste.

Day 19 Menu

Breakfast
Oatmeal with Walnuts and Blueberries
½ Raspberry Smoothie
Beverage of Choice

Lunch
Barley Cranberry Salad
Other 1/2 of Raspberry Smoothie
Beverage of Choice

Dinner
Salmon Shrimp Ceviche
Beverage of Choice

Salt/Sodium for the Day: If you are limiting sodium to 1500 mg./day then you should not add salt to food or in cooking today beyond what is already in the recipes. If limiting to 2300 mg/day you can add an additional 3/8 tsp. salt to food or in cooking today.

Calories for the Day: If not restricting calories to 1600 per day you have the options of extra Oatmeal at breakfast, a larger portion Barley Cranberry salad at Lunch and extra avocado at Dinner.

Recipes

Breakfast: Steel Cut Oatmeal with Blueberries and Walnuts, ½ of Raspberry Smoothie.

Oatmeal recipe: Makes 1 serving.

¼ cup steel cut oats (may substitute rolled oats if you prefer)
1 cup unsweetened almond milk
1/4 tsp. ground cinnamon, or to taste
1/8 tsp. ground ginger, or to taste
1/2 tsp. vanilla, or to taste
1 tsp. honey or maple syrup
½ cup blueberries
1 Tbsp. walnuts, chopped
1 Tbsp. flaxseed (optional, just adds 37 calories and has lots of
    health benefits)

Prepare oatmeal according to package directions using almond milk instead of water. Mix in cinnamon, ginger, vanilla, honey (or maple syrup) and flaxseed. Once cooked to desired consistency add blueberries and walnuts and serve immediately.

Raspberry Smoothie recipe: To be divided to drink ½ at breakfast and ½ at lunch.

Blend all of the following ingredients in a high-speed blender until smooth:
½ cup of unsweetened Almond Milk (Calcium calculation based on
    using almond milk containing 300 mg Calcium per 8 ounces
    or 30% of the Calcium RDA. If using a product higher than 300
    mg. then use only amount of Almond Milk required for 300 mg.
    Calcium and use water for the rest of the liquid).
¾ cup plain nonfat Greek Yogurt (containing 300 mg Calcium per 1
    cup serving. Nutrition label will say 30% of the RDA for Calcium)
1 cup raw kale
1/2 cup frozen or fresh raspberries (may substitute another fruit for
    raspberries)
1 medium banana
1 Tbsp. flaxseed (optional, just adds 37 calories and has lots of
    health benefits)

Add additional water or ice cubes if a different consistency is desired.

If you have parsley or other greens that you need to use before they go bad then add them to your smoothie – don't let them go to waste.

Lunch: Barley Cranberry Salad (Leftover Salad from Day 16), Other half of Raspberry Smoothie.

Dinner: Salmon Shrimp Ceviche with Tortillas Chips and ½ half Avocado (if limiting calories to 1600 today then leave out avocado).

Salmon Shrimp Ceviche Recipe: Serves 4. Make enough for lunch tomorrow.

½ pound raw salmon (preferably wild) cut in ½ inch cubes
1 cup lime juice
½ pound small cooked shrimp, peeled and deveined
1 medium red onion, chopped
1 jalapeno pepper, finely chopped
¼ cup chopped fresh cilantro
2 tomatoes, chopped
¼ tsp. sea salt
½ tsp. ground cumin
¼ tsp. smoked paprika
¼ tsp. black pepper or to taste
2 Tbsp. olive oil

Put salmon in a medium size glass container. Cover with lime juice and refrigerate for at least 3 hours.

In medium bowl mix shrimp, red onion, jalapeno pepper, cilantro, tomatoes, salt, cumin, paprika, black pepper and olive oil. Add shrimp mixture to salmon and serve with avocado and Tortilla Chips.

Serve Tortilla chips made from whole grains (I use Central Market Organic Red Quinoa and Flaxseed Tortilla Chips purchased at Central Market, a Texas grocery store chain. Another option is Multi grain Wasa crispbreads. If you are limiting calories to 1600 per day then allow 235 calories worth of chips and if restricting sodium to 1500 mg. per day then allow up to 388 mg. sodium for the chips).

Day 20 Menu

Breakfast
Mushroom and Tomato Omelet
Whole Grain Toast
Beverage of Choice

Snack anytime during the Day
Cherry Smoothie

Lunch
Salmon and Shrimp Ceviche
Avocado
Beverage of Choice

Dinner
Spinach Enchiladas
Banana Soft Serve "Ice Cream"
Beverage of Choice

Salt/Sodium for the Day: If you are limiting sodium to 1500 mg./day then you should not use the salt called for on the omelet or on the Spinach Enchiladas and you should use low sodium tomato sauce in the enchiladas. If limiting to 2300 mg./day then you should not add salt to food or in cooking today beyond what is already in the recipes.

Calories for the Day: If not restricting calories to 1600 per day you have the options of having a second slice of whole grain bread at Breakfast or you may have whole grain biscuits at Breakfast. You can also have jam on your toast (preferably 100% fruit jam). You may have an additional serving of Ceviche and Avocado at Lunch. You may have additional Enchiladas and Banana Soft Serve at Dinner.

Recipes:

Breakfast: Mushroom and Tomato Omelet with Whole Grain Toast or Biscuits.

Omelet Recipe:

Per Person: Heat 1/2 tsp. olive oil in skillet over medium heat. Add 1 cup sliced mushrooms and cook until tender. Add ½ cup chopped tomato to skillet. Cook 1 minute over medium heat. Add 1 tsp. fresh thyme or ½ tsp. dried thyme to skillet. Remove vegetable mixture from pan and keep warm. Heat ½ tsp. olive oil in skillet over low heat. In a bowl whisk together 2 eggs (may use 4 egg whites or 1 whole egg plus 2 egg whites instead), black pepper and light sprinkling of sea salt (if not restricting sodium to 1500 mg./day). Add eggs to skillet and cook omelet adding ½ mushroom tomato mixture once eggs are just done to one side of the omelet. Fold omelet in half and serve with remaining mushroom tomato mixture on top.

Snack anytime during the day: Cherry Smoothie

Cherry Smoothie recipe:

Blend all of the following ingredients in a high-speed blender until smooth:
1 cup of unsweetened Almond Milk (Calcium calculation based on
    using almond milk containing 300 mg Calcium per 8 ounces or
    30% of the Calcium RDA. If using a product higher than 300 mg.
    then use only amount of Almond Milk required for 300 mg.
    Calcium and use water for the rest of the liquid).
¼ cup plain nonfat Greek Yogurt (containing 300 mg Calcium per 1
    cup serving. Nutrition label will say 30% of the RDA for Calcium)
1 cup raw kale
1/2 cup frozen cherries (may substitute another fruit for cherries)
1 medium banana
1 Tbsp. flaxseed (optional, just adds 37 calories and has lots of
    health benefits)

Add additional water or ice cubes if a different consistency is desired.
If you have parsley or other greens that you need to use before they go bad then add them to your smoothie – don't let them go to waste.

Lunch: Ceviche (leftover from dinner last night), ½ avocado (calories are included in 1600) and chips.

Dinner: Spinach Enchiladas, Banana Soft Serve "Ice Cream".

Recipe for Spinach Enchiladas: Makes 8 enchiladas. Serving size is 2 enchiladas.   Make enough for Lunch tomorrow, too. Freeze any leftovers for another meal.

Preheat oven to 400° F.

1 tsp. plus 1/8 tsp. plus 1 Tbsp. olive oil - divided
16 cups fresh spinach
4 cloves garlic, finely chopped
½ tsp. sea salt – divided in half
1 Tbsp. fresh thyme, chopped finely or 1 tsp. dried thyme
¾ cup Jalapeno Jack Cheese, grated and divided (1/2 cup & ¼ cup)
1 cup cherry tomatoes
8 ounce can tomato sauce (low sodium if limiting sodium)
2 Tbsp. fresh oregano or 1 Tbsp. dried – divided in half
¼ tsp. chili powder
2 Tbsp. cilantro, chopped – divided in half
8 corn tortillas
1 zucchini, sliced bite size (substitute carrots or winter squash if
    zucchini not available)
4 ounces mushrooms, sliced
1 leek, chopped
1 jalapeno, chopped

Heat 1 tsp. olive oil in a large pot over medium heat. Sauté spinach and garlic in olive oil until spinach is just wilted. Mix in ¼ tsp. salt and 1 Tbsp. fresh thyme. Remove spinach mixture from pot and drain on paper or lint free cloth towels. In a small bowl, mix spinach with ½ cup of the cheese and set aside.

Mix cherry tomatoes with 1/8 tsp. olive oil. Spread on a parchment lined cookie sheet or pan and roast at 400° for 15 to 20 minutes or until tomatoes pop. Set aside. Lower oven temperature to 300° F.

In another small bowl mix tomato sauce, 1 Tbsp. fresh oregano, ¼ tsp. chili powder and 1 Tbsp. cilantro. Set aside.

Wrap corn tortillas in foil and warm 5 minutes in 300 degree oven or just until pliable. Do not overheat as they will become too crisp. Removing 1 warmed tortilla at a time, lay tortilla flat and put ¼ cup of spinach cheese mixture down the center of the tortilla and roll into a tube. Place seam side down in a pan that has been lightly greased with olive oil. Cover with tomato sauce mixture. Top with remaining ¼ cup cheese. Increase oven temperature to 350° and heat for 20 minutes or until warm.

While enchiladas are warming heat 1 Tbsp. olive oil in a large skillet. Sauté zucchini, mushrooms, leek and jalapeno in olive oil until tender. Add ¼ tsp. salt, 1 Tbsp. fresh oregano and 1 Tbsp. cilantro to vegetable mixture. Add roasted tomatoes and cook just until warmed. Serve vegetables on top of warm enchiladas.

Recipe for Banana Soft Serve:
Per serving:

1 Ripe Banana, peeled and sliced into 1 inch pieces, frozen
1 Tbsp. Almond Butter
1 Tbsp. Almond Milk
1 tsp. Maple syrup

Wrap banana slices in plastic wrap and freeze until hard. I keep frozen bananas in my freezer at all times for smoothies and soft serve.

In a high-speed blender, blend frozen banana slices, almond butter, almond milk and maple syrup. It should be the texture of soft serve ice cream. Eat immediately or freeze for a few minutes for a more frozen product.

Day 21 Menu

<u>Breakfast</u>
Apple Muffins
½ Mango Smoothie
Beverage of Choice

<u>Snack anytime during the Day</u>
Other ½ of Mango Smoothie

<u>Lunch</u>
Spinach Enchiladas
Citrus Parfait
Beverage of Choice

<u>Afternoon or Evening Snack</u>
Popcorn

<u>Dinner</u>
Salmon with Dill
Sautéed Mushrooms
Roasted Broccoli
Whole Grain Bread or Roll
Chocolate covered Strawberries
Beverage of Choice

Salt/Sodium for the Day: If you are limiting sodium to 1500 mg./day then you should not add salt to food or in cooking today beyond what is already in the recipes. If limiting to 2300 mg/day you can add an additional 3/8 tsp. salt to food or in cooking today.

Calories for the Day: If not restricting calories to 1600 per day you have the options of having a third muffin at Breakfast, extra enchiladas at Lunch, olive oil on Popcorn, an additional 2 ounce salmon and extra chocolate covered strawberries at Dinner.

<u>Recipes:</u>
<u>Breakfast:</u> 2 Apple Muffins, ½ Mango Smoothie

Apple Muffin Recipe: Makes 12 muffins (freeze leftovers for Day 25)

Preheat oven to 400° F.

1 cup whole wheat flour
¾ cup almond flour/meal
2 tsp. baking powder
¼ tsp. salt
½ tsp. cinnamon
½ tsp. cardamom (optional – an expensive spice but adds great flavor)
1 cup grated apple
1 egg
2 Tbsp. honey
¼ cup blackstrap molasses, preferably unsulphured
½ cup almond butter
1 cup almond milk

Mix flours, baking powder, salt, cinnamon and cardamom in large bowl. Add grated apple and mix to coat apple with flour mixture.

In small bowl lightly beat egg with fork. Mix in honey, molasses, almond butter, and almond milk. Add to dry ingredients and stir just until blended.

Prepare 12 muffin cups and divide batter evenly between muffin cups. Batter will come to the top of muffin cups. Bake at 400°F. for 15 to 20 minutes or until done.

Mango Smoothie recipe: To be divided to drink ½ at Breakfast and ½ as Snack anytime during the day.

Blend all of the following ingredients in a high-speed blender until smooth:
2/3 cup of unsweetened Almond Milk (Calcium calculation based on using almond milk containing 300 mg Calcium per 8 ounces or 30% of the Calcium RDA. If using a product higher than 300 mg. then use only amount of Almond Milk required for 300 mg. Calcium and use water for the rest of the liquid).

¼ cup plain nonfat Greek Yogurt (containing 300 mg Calcium per 1
   cup serving. Nutrition label will say 30% of the RDA for Calcium)
1 cup raw Spinach
1/2 cup frozen or fresh mango (may substitute another fruit for
   mango)
1 medium banana
1 Tbsp. flaxseed (optional, just adds 37 calories and has lots of
   health benefits)

Add additional water or ice cubes if a different consistency is
desired.
If you have parsley or other greens that you need to use before they
go bad then add them to your smoothie – don't let them go to waste.

Lunch: Spinach Enchiladas (leftover from yesterday dinner – 2 if
limiting calories to 1600/day), Citrus Parfait.

Citrus Parfait Recipe:

Per Person:
Mix ¼ cup Greek Yogurt with ½ tsp. honey. In parfait glass, or wine
glass layer yogurt mixture with ½ orange in sections, ½ grapefruit in
sections and 1 Tbsp. sunflower seeds. Throw in some fresh mint
leaves if you like.

Snack: Popcorn (3 cups if limiting to 1600 calories/day).

Dinner: Salmon with Dill, Sautéed Mushrooms, Roasted Broccoli, 1
Whole grain bread or roll and Chocolate Covered Strawberries.

Salmon Recipe:
Preheat oven to 400° F. if not grilling salmon.

4 ounces raw salmon (preferably wild) per person plus 4 ounces raw
   salmon per person for lunch salad tomorrow
1 tsp. Fresh Dill, or ½ tsp. dried dill
½ cup white wine or water if not grilling

Sprinkle Dill evenly on raw salmon. Cook on grill until just done.
Or put in baking dish, add white wine or water and bake uncovered
for 12 to 15 minutes or until just done. Avoid overcooking which will
dry the salmon out. Refrigerate 4 ounces for salad tomorrow and
eat the other 4 ounces for dinner.

Roasted Broccoli Recipe:
Preheat oven to 400° F.
Per person:
1 cup Broccoli, washed and cut into bite size florets
1 tsp. olive oil
Black pepper to taste
Lemon juice/wedges, if desired

Place Broccoli in bowl. Add olive oil to coat Broccoli (if you use your hands it will coat more evenly). Add pepper and any other desired herbs or spices. Evenly distribute broccoli in a single layer on a parchment lined baking pan. Bake at 400° F. for 10 to 15 minutes or until done, stirring once after 5 minutes and again as needed. Squeeze fresh lemon juice over before serving.

Sautéed Mushrooms Recipe:
Per person:
1 cup mushrooms, sliced
1 tsp. olive oil
¼ cup White wine or water
1 tsp. fresh or ½ tsp. dried Thyme

In skillet heat olive oil over medium heat. Add mushrooms and cook for 2 minutes, stirring frequently. Add water or white wine and continue to cook until water or wine has cooked off and mushrooms are tender. Sprinkle with Thyme and serve.

See Day 9 for Chocolate Covered Strawberries Recipe

Day 22 Menu

Breakfast
Almond Toast
½ Strawberry Smoothie
Beverage of Choice

Snack anytime during the day
Other ½ of Strawberry Smoothie

Lunch
Salmon Salad
Whole Grain Roll or Bread
Beverage of Choice

Dinner
Roasted Garlic, Lentil and Chard Soup
Whole Grain Roll or Bread
Pear or Fruit of Choice with Chocolate
Beverage of Choice

Salt/Sodium for the Day: If you are limiting sodium to 1500 mg./day do not add additional salt to food or in cooking today beyond what is already in the recipes. If limiting to 2300 mg/day you can add an additional 3/8 tsp. salt to food or in cooking today.

Calories for the Day: If not restricting calories to 1600 per day you have the options of having 2 slices Almond Toast at Breakfast, having more Salmon salad at Lunch and more Soup at Dinner.

Recipes:

Breakfast: Almond Toast, ½ of Strawberry Smoothie.

Spread 2 Tbsp. almond butter on 1 slice toasted whole grain bread. Prepare Strawberry Smoothie.

Strawberry Smoothie recipe: To be divided to drink ½ at breakfast and ½ as snack anytime during the day.

Blend all of the following ingredients in a high-speed blender until smooth:

1-¼ cups of unsweetened Almond Milk (Calcium calculation based on using almond milk containing 300 mg Calcium per 8 ounces or 30% of the Calcium RDA. If using a product higher than 300 mg. then use only amount of Almond Milk required for 300 mg. Calcium and use water for the rest of the liquid).

1 cup raw kale

1 cup frozen or fresh strawberries (may substitute another fruit for strawberries)

1 medium banana

1 Tbsp. flaxseed (optional, just adds 37 calories and has lots of health benefits)

Add additional water or ice cubes if a different consistency is desired.

If you have parsley or other greens that you need to use before they go bad then add them to your smoothie – don't let them go to waste.

Lunch: Salmon Salad, 1 whole grain roll or bread.

Salmon Salad Recipe:

For each person toss the following salad ingredients together:

1 cup raw spinach

1 cup mixed greens

½ cup red cabbage, shredded

1/4th of a cucumber, sliced

½ cup roasted beets, cooled (Coat bite size slices of beets in ½ tsp. olive oil and distribute evenly over a parchment lined baking sheet. Bake at 400° F. until tender)

Add ½ cup Yogurt Dill Dressing per serving (recipe on next page)

Top with 4 ounces salmon, leftover from dinner yesterday.

Yogurt Dill Dressing - Combine the following ingredients in a jar or small bowl until well blended:

1 cup plain nonfat Yogurt
¼ tsp. kosher or sea salt
½ tsp. paprika
¼ tsp. garlic powder
½ tsp. dried dill weed or 1 ½ tsp. fresh dill
¼ tsp. onion powder
2 Tbsp. fresh lemon juice
1 Tbsp. olive oil
1/16 tsp. cayenne pepper

Dinner: Roasted Garlic, Lentil and Chard Soup, 1 whole grain roll or slice of bread, Fresh Pear or fruit of choice, 2 squares dark chocolate.

Roasted Garlic Lentil and Chard Soup Recipe: Serves 6. Make enough for lunch tomorrow.

Preheat oven to 325°F.

1 whole garlic head
1 tsp. plus 1 Tbsp. olive oil - divided
1 onion, chopped
1 cup diced carrot
2 stalks celery, chopped
2 quarts water
2 cups dried brown or black lentils, sorted and rinsed
1 Tbsp. fresh thyme, chopped or 1 tsp. dried thyme
2 bay leaves
½ cup chopped fresh flat leaf parsley
1 tsp. ground cumin
½ tsp. ground coriander
¼ tsp. cayenne pepper, or to taste
8 cups shredded Swiss Chard
½ tsp. sea salt
1 Tbsp. fresh lemon juice
¾ cup nonfat plain Greek yogurt
¼ tsp. smoked paprika

Remove papery skin from garlic head but do not separate the garlic cloves from the head. Cut off tip ends of cloves so it will be easier to squeeze garlic out. Place garlic in small oven safe bowl or pan. Pour 1 tsp. olive oil over garlic head coating all the cloves and cover with foil. Cook at 325° until garlic is soft when pressed, about 30 to 40 minutes. Remove from oven and allow to cool. Once cool enough to work with squeeze garlic out of skins and set aside to add to soup later.

Heat 1 Tbsp. olive oil in large pot over medium heat. Add onion, carrot and celery and cook 5 minutes, stirring frequently. Add water, lentils, thyme, bay leaves, parsley, cumin, coriander and cayenne pepper.
Bring to boil, reduce heat and simmer 25 to 30 minutes or until lentils are tender. Remove bay leaves. Add roasted garlic, Swiss chard, ½ tsp. salt and lemon juice to lentils and let simmer another 5 to 10 minutes or until chard is tender.

Mix yogurt with smoked paprika in small bowl.

You may serve soup as is or if you want a blended soup then in batches transfer soup to blender and blend until smooth. CAUTION: Blending hot liquids will cause the lid of the blender to explode off. To avoid burns and a mess only fill the blender half full (blend in batches) and vent the lid. Many blenders have a lid with a center piece that comes out. Remove the center piece. Cover lid with kitchen towel to avoid sprays but still allow steam to escape.

Serve soup in bowls with 2 Tbsp. of Greek Yogurt Paprika mixture on top of each serving.

Day 23 Menu

Breakfast
Granola with Blackberries
Beverage of Choice

Snack anytime during the day
Peach Smoothie

Lunch
Roasted Garlic, Lentil and Chard Soup
Whole grain roll or bread
Apple or fruit of choice
Beverage of Choice

Dinner
Whole Grain Pasta with Portabella Mushrooms
Green Salad with Blueberries
Beverage of Choice

Salt/Sodium for the Day: If you are limiting sodium to 1500 mg./day then you should not add salt to food or in cooking today beyond what is already in the recipes. If limiting to 2300 mg/day you can add an additional 3/8 tsp. salt to food or in cooking today.

Calories for the Day: If not restricting calories to 1600 per day you have the options of having more Granola at Breakfast, extra soup at Lunch and more salad and a serving of bread at Dinner.

Recipes

Breakfast: ½ cup Granola with ¾ cup Non-fat Plain Greek Yogurt, 1/2 cup blackberries, or fruit of choice and 1 tsp. honey or maple syrup if desired. May substitute unsweetened Almond Milk or a non-dairy yogurt for Greek Yogurt. Use the Granola recipe from Day 2.

Snack anytime during the day: Peach Smoothie

Peach Smoothie recipe: To drink as a snack anytime during the day.

Blend all of the following ingredients in a high-speed blender until smooth:
1 ¼ cup of unsweetened Almond Milk (Calcium calculation based on using almond milk containing 300 mg Calcium per 8 ounces or 30% of the Calcium RDA. If using a product higher than 300 mg. then use only amount of Almond Milk required for 300 mg. Calcium and use water for the rest of the liquid).
1 cup raw kale
1 cup frozen or fresh peach (may substitute another fruit for peach)
1 medium banana
1 Tbsp. flaxseed (optional, just adds 37 calories and has lots of health benefits)

Add additional water or ice cubes if a different consistency is desired.
If you have parsley or other greens that you need to use before they go bad then add them to your smoothie – don't let them go to waste.

Lunch: Roasted Garlic, Lentil and Chard Soup (leftover from last night), 1 slice whole grain bread or roll, 1 Apple or fruit of choice.

Dinner: Whole grain pasta with Portabella Mushrooms, Green Salad with Blueberries.

Whole Grain Pasta with Portabella Mushrooms Recipe:

Per Serving:
1 tsp. olive oil
1 garlic clove, minced
1 Portabella mushroom, sliced in to ½ inch lengthwise pieces
1 tsp. fresh Thyme, chopped or ½ tsp. dried Thyme

1/8 tsp. sea salt
1/8 tsp. Cayenne pepper or to taste
1 cup cooked whole grain Pasta
2 Tbsp. Parmesan Cheese

In skillet heat olive oil over medium heat. Add Portabella mushroom and garlic and cook until mushroom is tender. Add Thyme, salt, and cayenne pepper to mushroom garlic mixture. Serve over warm pasta and top with Parmesan Cheese.

Green Salad with Blueberries Recipe:

For each person toss the following salad ingredients together:

1 cup raw Spinach
1 cup mixed Greens
1 Tbsp. red onion, chopped

Add 1 Tbsp. Raspberry Vinaigrette (see recipe below). May have more if not restricting calories to 1600.

To make Raspberry Vinaigrette put the following ingredients in a jar and shake until well blended:

3 Tbsp. Raspberry Vinegar
3 Tbsp. Honey
1 Tbsp. plain nonfat Greek Yogurt
1 tsp. Dijon Mustard
¼ cup Olive or Walnut oil

Top each serving with:
¼ cup blueberries
1 Tbsp. blue cheese.

Day 24 Menu

Breakfast
Oatmeal with Dried Fruit and Walnuts
½ Blueberry Smoothie
Beverage of Choice

Snack anytime during the day
Other ½ of Blueberry Smoothie

Lunch
Sweet Potato Quinoa Salad
Raspberries with Yogurt
Beverage of Choice

Dinner
Fish with Chutney
Snow Peas with Almonds
Spaghetti Squash
Whole Grain Bread or Roll
Grapes or Fruit of Choice
Beverage of Choice

Salt/Sodium for the Day: If you are limiting sodium to 1500 mg./day then you should not add salt to food or in cooking today beyond what is already in the recipes. If limiting to 2300 mg/day you can add an additional 3/8 tsp. salt to food or in cooking today.

Calories for the Day: If not restricting calories to 1600 per day you have the options of having more Oatmeal at Breakfast, extra salad and whole grain bread or roll at Lunch and 2 ounces more fish at Dinner.

Recipes
Breakfast: Steel Cut Oatmeal with Dried Fruit & Walnut, ½ of Blueberry Smoothie

Oatmeal recipe: Makes 1 serving.

¼ cup steel cut oats (may substitute rolled oats if you prefer)
1 cup unsweetened almond milk
1/4 tsp. ground cinnamon, or to taste
1/8 tsp. ground ginger, or to taste
1/2 tsp. vanilla, or to taste
1 Tbsp. raisins
4 dried apricots, chopped
1 tsp. honey or maple syrup
1 Tbsp. walnuts, chopped
1 Tbsp. flaxseed (optional, just adds 37 calories and has lots of
    health benefits)

Prepare oatmeal according to package directions using almond milk instead of water. Mix in cinnamon, ginger, vanilla, raisins, apricots, honey (or maple syrup), walnuts and flaxseed.

Blueberry Smoothie recipe: To be divided to drink ½ at breakfast and ½ as snack.

Blend all of the following ingredients in a high-speed blender until smooth:
3/4 cup of unsweetened Almond Milk (Calcium calculation based on
    using almond milk containing 300 mg Calcium per 8 ounces or
    30% of the Calcium RDA. If using a product higher than 300 mg.
    then use only amount of Almond Milk required for 300 mg.
    Calcium and use water for the rest of the liquid).
¼ cup plain nonfat Greek Yogurt (containing 300 mg Calcium per 1
    cup serving. Nutrition label will say 30% of the RDA for Calcium)
1 cup raw kale
1/2 cup frozen or fresh blueberries (may substitute another fruit for
    blueberries)
1 medium banana
1 Tbsp. flaxseed (optional, just adds 37 calories and has lots of
    health benefits)

Add additional water or ice cubes if a different consistency is desired.

If you have parsley or other greens that you need to use before they go bad then add them to your smoothie – don't let them go to waste.

Lunch: Sweet Potato Quinoa Salad, ½ cup Raspberries with ½ cup Greek Yogurt mixed with 1 tsp. honey.

Sweet Potato Quinoa Salad Recipe: Makes 2 servings. Make enough for lunch on Day 26 as well so double recipe if cooking for two.

Preheat oven to 400°F

2 cups cooked quinoa
1 large sweet potato
1 tsp. olive oil
½ cup fresh sage leaves
Juice of 2 lemons
¼ cup pumpkin seeds
¼ cup raisins
1/8 tsp. kosher or sea salt

Prepare quinoa according to package directions.

Cut sweet potato in to bite size pieces. Coat sweet potato with olive oil. Mix in sage leaves. Evenly distribute sweet potato and sage leaves in a single layer on a parchment lined baking sheet. Roast sweet potato sage mixture 20 to 25 minutes at 400° F. or until done. Remove from oven, add lemon juice and let cook slightly.

In large bowl mix quinoa, sweet potato mixture, pumpkin seeds, raisins and salt. Serve cold or at room temperature.

Dinner: Grilled or Baked Fish with Chutney, Snow Peas with Almonds, Spaghetti Squash, Whole Grain Bread or Roll, 1 cup Grapes or fruit of choice.

Fish with Chutney Recipe:

Preheat oven to 400°F. if not grilling Fish.

Per person:
4 ounces fish preferably sustainable such as Arctic Char (farmed),
    Tilapia (Ecuador & US), Catfish (US) or Pacific Halibut (US). Go
    to www.seafoodwatch.org for sustainable fish purchasing
    guidelines. You can also look for fish with the Marine
    Stewardship Council Blue eco-label in your grocery store.
½ cup white wine or water if not grilling
2 Tbsp. Chutney (preferably one with fruit, not sugar, as the first
    ingredient)

Spread chutney on top of fish.

Cook fish on grill until just done. Or put in baking dish, add white
wine or water and bake uncovered for 12 to 15 minutes or until just
done. Avoid overcooking which will dry the fish out.

Snow Peas Recipe: For each serving heat ½ tsp. olive oil in skillet
over medium heat. Sauté ½ cup snow peas for about 3 minutes.
Mix in 1/8 tsp. sea salt. Sprinkle 1 Tbsp. almonds on top of snow
peas.

Spaghetti Squash Recipe: Serving size is 1 cup of squash.

Preheat oven to 400° F.

Cut squash in half. Remove seeds. Place cut side down in a
baking dish lightly oiled with olive oil. Bake at 400° until tender
when pierced with a fork, about 30 to 40 minutes. Remove from
oven. Pull a fork lengthwise through the flesh to pull off spaghetti
like long strands. You can simply add olive oil, chopped parsley,
salt and pepper and serve or for every 1 cup squash heat ½ tsp.
olive oil and 1 minced garlic clove over medium heat in skillet. Add
squash to skillet. Mix 1/8 tsp. salt, black pepper to taste and 1 tsp.
chopped Italian leaf parsley per 1 cup serving into the squash and
serve. If you can afford the extra calories drizzle a little high quality
olive oil over the top.

Day 25 Menu

Breakfast
Apple Muffins
½ of Cherry Smoothie
Beverage of Choice

Snack anytime during the day
½ of Cherry Smoothie

Lunch
Hummus
Broccoli & Cauliflower
Whole Grain Crackers or Bread
Other ½ of Cherry Smoothie
Beverage of Choice

Dinner
Chicken Breast
Sautéed Carrots
Citrus and Green Salad with Lemon Maple Dressing
Beverage of Choice

Salt/Sodium for the Day: If you are limiting sodium to 1500 mg./day then you can add 1/16 tsp. salt to food or in cooking today beyond what is already in the recipes. If limiting to 2300 mg/day you can add an additional 3/8 tsp. salt to food or in cooking today.

Calories for the Day: If not restricting calories to 1600 per day you have the options of having 2 extra muffins at Breakfast and adding Almond Butter to toasted muffins, extra hummus at Lunch, more salad, salad dressing, 2 oz. more chicken and a serving of whole grain bread at Dinner.

Recipes
Breakfast: Apple Muffins (leftover from Day 21) with ½ of Cherry Smoothie.

Cherry Smoothie recipe: To be divided to drink ½ at breakfast and ½ as snack anytime during the day.

Blend all of the following ingredients in a high-speed blender until smooth:

2/3 cup of unsweetened Almond Milk (Calcium calculation based on using almond milk containing 300 mg Calcium per 8 ounces or 30% of the Calcium RDA. If using a product higher than 300 mg. then use only amount of Almond Milk required for 300 mg. Calcium and use water for the rest of the liquid).

1 cup plain nonfat Greek Yogurt (containing 300 mg Calcium per 1 cup serving. Nutrition label will say 30% of the RDA for Calcium)

1 cup frozen cherries

1 cup frozen beets

1 medium banana

1 Tbsp. flaxseed (optional, just adds 37 calories and has lots of health benefits)

Add additional water or ice cubes if a different consistency is desired.

If you have parsley or other greens that you need to use before they go bad then add them to your smoothie – don't let them go to waste.

Lunch: 1/2 cup Hummus with raw Broccoli (as much as you like) and Cauliflower (as much as you like) plus 6 whole grain crackers or a slice of whole grain bread (I like Flackers – crackers made from flax seeds or try Wasa Multigrain Flatbreads). Other half of Cherry Smoothie.

Dinner: Chicken Breast (serving size 4 oz. raw), Sautéed Carrots, Citrus and Green Salad with Lemon Maple Dressing.

Grill or Cook chicken breasts according to your favorite method. Here are some options:

Brine: 1 Tbsp. salt dissolved in 1 ½ cups water for every 6 to 8 ounce chicken breast

Dissolve salt in water and submerge chicken in brine. Cover and refrigerate for at least 30 minutes or up to 1 hour. Remove chicken from brine and dry chicken on paper or lint free cloth towel. Spray or lightly brush chicken breasts with olive oil and desired seasonings. Grill, bake or sauté.

Overcooking chicken breasts results in dry tough chicken. For even cooking you can pound the chicken breasts to flatten them to an even thickness.
Yogurt marinade option:
Marinate each 6 to 8 ounce chicken breast in ¼ cup plain nonfat yogurt over night.
For glazed chicken Cook's Illustrated (Sept/Oct 2013) recommends lightly sprinkling chicken breasts with a combination of nonfat dry milk powder (2 tsp. for four 6 to 8 ounce chicken breasts) and pepper (1/4 tsp.) then lightly spraying with oil. Coat both sides. When grilling cook for 2 minutes over hot grill, flip chicken, brush with desired glaze and cook another 2 minutes. Continue process of cooking 2 minutes, brushing with glaze and flipping until done (160° F and around). After second flip or 6 minutes in to process move chicken to cooler side of grill. Once done allow chicken to stand for 5 minutes prior to serving. Make a glaze from pureed fruit or use fruit jam (preferably one with fruit as the first ingredient). Maple syrup also makes a good quick glaze.

En Papillote – Preheat the oven to 375° F. Season chicken breast with olive oil and desired seasonings. Cut 15 inch squares of parchment paper (or aluminum foil). Fold square in half to make a crease in center of paper or foil. Lay chicken breast just to one side of the crease. Seal packets by loosely folding the other half of the paper or foil over the chicken. Turn up edges of paper or foil in ½ inch fold on all open edges. Smooth fold to make a sharp crease and double fold for a secure seal. Press smooth again. Bake packets on baking sheet for 15 to 25 minutes at 375° F., depending on thickness of chicken, until done (160° F). Allow chicken to stand for 5 minutes prior to serving.

Sautéed Carrots Recipe: Cut carrots into sticks or strips (1 cup per person). Heat 1 tsp. olive oil per serving in skillet over medium heat. Sauté carrots until tender. Can finish with balsamic vinegar if desired.

Citrus and Green Salad with Lemon Maple Dressing:

Per Person:
2 cups mixed greens
½ orange, in sections
½ grapefruit, in sections
2 Tbsp. Lemon Maple Dressing

To make Lemon Maple Dressing put the following ingredients in a jar and shake until well blended:

1 Tbsp. Dijon Mustard
¼ cup fresh lemon juice
2 Tbsp. maple syrup
¼ cup olive oil

Mix greens with Lemon Maple Dressing.   Arrange on salad plate. Top with orange and grapefruit sections.

Day 26 Menu

Breakfast
Granola with Blueberries
Beverage of Choice

Lunch
Sweet Potato Quinoa Salad
½ Raspberry Smoothie
Beverage of Choice

Dinner
Black Bean Tacos
Other ½ Raspberry Smoothie
Orange or Fruit of Choice
Beverage of Choice

Salt/Sodium for the Day: If you are limiting sodium to 1500 mg./day then you should not add salt to food or in cooking today beyond what is already in the recipes. If limiting to 2300 mg/day you can add an additional 3/8 tsp. salt to food or in cooking today.

Calories for the Day: If not restricting calories to 1600 per day you have the options of more Granola and fruit at Breakfast, having extra salad at Lunch and more avocado at Dinner.

Recipes

Breakfast: ½ cup Granola with ¾ cup Non-fat Plain Greek Yogurt, 1/2 cup Blueberries or fruit of choice and 1 tsp. honey or maple syrup if desired. May substitute unsweetened Almond Milk or a non-dairy yogurt for Greek Yogurt. Use the Granola recipe from Day 2.

Sweet Potato Quinoa Salad: Leftover from Day 24, ½ Raspberry Smoothie.

Raspberry Smoothie recipe: To be divided to drink ½ at Lunch and ½ at Dinner.

Blend all of the following ingredients in a high-speed blender until smooth:

3/4 cup of unsweetened Almond Milk (Calcium calculation based on using almond milk containing 300 mg Calcium per 8 ounces or 30% of the Calcium RDA. If using a product higher than 300 mg. then use only amount of Almond Milk required for 300 mg. Calcium and use water for the rest of the liquid).

3/4 cup plain nonfat Greek Yogurt (containing 300 mg Calcium per 1 cup serving. Nutrition label will say 30% of the RDA for Calcium)

1 cup raw kale

1 cup frozen or fresh raspberries (may substitute another fruit for raspberry)

1 medium banana

1 Tbsp. flaxseed (optional, just adds 37 calories and has lots of health benefits)

Add additional water or ice cubes if a different consistency is desired.

If you have parsley or other greens that you need to use before they go bad then add them to your smoothie – don't let them go to waste.

Dinner: 2 Black Bean Tacos, other ½ of Raspberry Smoothie, Orange or Fruit of choice.

Black Bean Tacos Recipe: Makes 4 Tacos (make enough to have 2 tomorrow for lunch)

Preheat oven to 350°F.

1 15 oz. can No salt added Black Beans or 1 3/4 cups cooked black
   beans, drained. I like Eden No Salt Added canned beans with
   BPA free lining or try Whole Foods 365 Organic No salt added
   beans that are packed in cartons. If you have time cook your
   own from dried beans.
1 garlic clove, minced
¼ tsp. Epazote (optional)
½ tsp. Mexican Oregano
¼ tsp. ground cumin
2 Tbsp. Cilantro, chopped
1/8 tsp. chili powder
1/8 tsp. cayenne pepper
1/8 tsp. smoked paprika
1/8 tsp. sea salt
½ cup cherry tomatoes, cut in half
1 tsp. olive oil
2 Tbsp. chopped onion
4 Whole Grain Flour Tortillas (or Corn)
¼ cup cheddar Cheese
1/2 Avocado
Salsa (optional)

In small bowl mix black beans (drained), garlic, epazote, oregano, cumin, cilantro, chili powder, cayenne pepper, paprika, salt and cherry tomatoes.

Wrap flour tortillas in foil and heat in 350° F oven. Don't overheat, which causes them to dry out and harden.

In small skillet heat olive oil. Sauté onion until just tender, 2 to 3 minutes. Add black bean mixture and stir frequently until well heated.

Serve black bean mixture in warm tortillas with 1 Tbsp. cheddar cheese per taco and 1/8th avocado per taco. Can add salsa if desired.

Day 27 Menu

Breakfast
Blueberry Muffins
½ Strawberry Smoothie
Beverage of Choice

Lunch
Black Bean Tacos
Other ½ Strawberry Smoothie
Beverage of Choice

Dinner
Fish in Verde Sauce
Roasted Cauliflower
Arugula, Endive, Radicchio Salad
Apple or Fruit of Choice
Beverage of Choice

Salt/Sodium for the Day: If you are limiting sodium to 1500 mg./day then you should not add salt to food or in cooking today beyond what is already in the recipes and today you will need to use corn tortillas or low sodium flour tortillas for the Black Bean Tacos at Lunch. If limiting to 2300 mg/day you can add an additional 1/8 tsp. salt to food or in cooking today and you don't need to use low sodium tortillas.

Calories for the Day: If not restricting calories to 1600 per day you have the options of having extra avocado at Lunch, extra salad dressing and a whole grain roll or slice of bread at Dinner.

Recipes:
Breakfast: 2 Blueberry Muffins, ½ Strawberry Smoothie.

Blueberry Muffins Recipe: Makes 12 muffins (Freeze some for another Breakfast)
Preheat oven to 400° F.

1 cup whole wheat flour
½ cup almond flour/meal
½ cup teff flour
2 tsp. baking powder
¼ tsp. salt
½ tsp. ground cinnamon
1 ½ cups blueberries
2 eggs
3 Tbsp. honey
2 Tbsp. molasses
½ cup almond butter
1 cup almond milk
½ tsp. vanilla

Mix flours, baking powder, salt and cinnamon in large bowl. Add blueberries and mix to coat blueberries with flour mixture.

In small bowl lightly beat eggs with fork. Mix in honey, molasses, almond butter, almond milk and vanilla. Add to dry ingredients and stir just until blended.

Prepare 12 muffin cups and divide batter evenly between muffin cups. Batter will come to the top of the muffin cups. Bake at 400°F. for 15 minutes or until done.

Strawberry Smoothie recipe: To be divided to drink ½ at Breakfast and ½ at Lunch.

Blend all of the following ingredients in a high-speed blender until smooth:
1 cup of unsweetened Almond Milk (Calcium calculation based on using almond milk containing 300 mg Calcium per 8 ounces or 30% of the Calcium RDA. If using a product higher than 300 mg. then use only amount of Almond Milk required for 300 mg. Calcium and use water for the rest of the liquid).
1/2 cup plain nonfat Greek Yogurt (containing 300 mg Calcium per 1

cup serving. Nutrition label will say 30% of the RDA for Calcium)
1 cup raw kale
1 cup frozen or fresh strawberries (may substitute another fruit for strawberries)
1 medium banana
1 Tbsp. flaxseed (optional, just adds 37 calories and has lots of
     health benefits)

Add additional water or ice cubes if a different consistency is desired.
If you have parsley or other greens that you need to use before they go bad then add them to your smoothie – don't let them go to waste.

Lunch: 2 Black Bean Tacos (leftover from last nights dinner), Other ½ of Strawberry Smoothie.

Dinner: Fish in Verde Sauce, Roasted Cauliflower, Arugula, Endive, Radicchio Salad, Apple or Fruit of choice.

Fish in Verde Sauce Recipe:

Preheat oven to 400°F. if not grilling Fish.

Per person:
4 ounces fish preferably sustainable such as Arctic Char (farmed),
     Tilapia (Ecuador & US), Catfish (US) or Pacific Halibut (US).   Go
     to www.seafoodwatch.org for sustainable fish purchasing
     guidelines.   You can also look for fish with the Marine
     Stewardship Council Blue eco-label in your grocery store.
½ cup white wine or water if not grilling
¼ cup Verde sauce (purchase premade or make your own)

Spread Verde Sauce on top of fish.

Cook fish on grill until just done. Or put in baking dish, add white wine or water and bake uncovered for 12 to 15 minutes or until just done. Avoid overcooking which will dry the fish out.

Roasted Cauliflower Recipe: Don't just use the white, try some of the colored cauliflower & mix them for a colorful dish.

Preheat oven to 400° F.

Per person:
1 cup cauliflower, washed and cut into bite size florets
1 tsp. olive oil
Black pepper to taste
Lemon juice/wedges, if desired

Place cauliflower in bowl. Add olive oil to coat cauliflower (if you use your hands it will coat more evenly). Add pepper and any other desired herbs or spices like cardamom, red chili flakes, cilantro, coriander, cumin, curry, dill, garlic powder, paprika, saffron, thyme or turmeric. Cumin would be good with the Fish. Evenly distribute cauliflower in a single layer on a parchment lined baking pan. Bake at 400° F. for 35 to 45 minutes or until soft and browned, stirring once after 10 minutes and again as needed.

Salad Recipe: May substitute other greens if you prefer milder greens

Per person mix:
1 cup Arugula
1/4 cup Radicchio, shredded
¼ cup Endive
2 Tbsp. Balsamic Vinaigrette

To make Balsamic Vinaigrette put the following ingredients in a jar and shake until well blended:

3 Tbsp. Balsamic Vinegar
3 Tbsp. Honey
1 Tbsp. Greek Yogurt
1 tsp. Dijon Mustard
¼ cup Olive or Walnut oil

Top each salad with 2 Tbsp. Goat Cheese

Day 28 Menu

Breakfast
Spinach Omelet
Whole Grain Toast
Orange Grapefruit Salad
Beverage of Choice

Snack Anytime during the Day
½ Mango Smoothie

Lunch
Shrimp Cocktail
Apple or Fruit of Choice
Other 1/2 of Mango Smoothie
Beverage of Choice

Dinner
Pork Tenderloin in Apricot Glaze
Carrots and Green Beans with Almonds
Mashed Potatoes
Beverage of Choice

Salt/Sodium for the Day: If you are limiting sodium to 1500 mg./day then you should not add salt to food or in cooking today beyond what is already in the recipes. If limiting to 2300 mg/day you can add an additional 3/8 tsp. salt to food or in cooking today.

Calories for the Day: If not restricting calories to 1600 per day you have the options of adding a second slice of whole grain toast with jam or having whole grain biscuits (2) with jam at Breakfast, adding avocado chunks to your Shrimp cocktail at Lunch, and having a whole grain roll or bread at Dinner.

Recipes:

Breakfast: Spinach Mushroom Omelet, 1 slice Whole Grain Toast with 1 Tbsp. 100% fruit jam, fruit salad made from ½ orange and ½ grapefruit per person.

Spinach Mushroom Omelet recipe:

Make each omelet with:
1 ½ tsp. olive oil, divided
½ cup mushrooms
2 cups spinach
2 eggs (can substitute 4 egg whites or 1 whole egg and 2 egg
   whites)
Black pepper to taste
2 Tbsp. Monterey jack cheese

In skillet over medium heat sauté mushrooms in ½ tsp. olive oil until tender. Remove from skillet and keep warm. Heat another ½ tsp. olive oil over medium heat in skillet. Add spinach to skillet and cook until just wilted. Remove spinach from pan and keep warm. Whisk eggs with pepper in small bowl. Heat remaining ½ tsp. olive oil in skillet over low heat. Add eggs and prepare omelet, adding cheese and spinach just as omelet sets. Fold omelet over, top with mushrooms and serve.

Mango Smoothie recipe: To be divided to drink ½ at lunch and half as a snack anytime during the day.

Blend all of the following ingredients in a high-speed blender until smooth:
1 ½ cup of unsweetened Almond Milk (Calcium calculation based on
   using almond milk containing 300 mg Calcium per 8 ounces or
   30% of the Calcium RDA. If using a product higher than 300 mg.
   then use only amount of Almond Milk required for 300 mg.
   Calcium and use water for the rest of the liquid).
2 cups raw kale
1 cup frozen or fresh mango (may substitute another fruit for
   mango)
1 medium banana
1 Tbsp. flaxseed (optional, just adds 37 calories and has lots of
   health benefits)

Add additional water or ice cubes if a different consistency is desired.

If you have parsley or other greens that you need to use before they go bad then add them to your smoothie – don't let them go to waste.

Lunch: Shrimp Cocktail, ½ Mango Smoothie, Apple or fruit of choice.

Shrimp Cocktail Recipe: Makes 2 servings

6 ounces cooked shrimp
12 cherry tomatoes cut in half
2 jalapeno peppers, finely chopped (use less if you like less heat)
2 Tbsp. chopped cilantro
½ cup pineapple chunks or tidbits, drained if from a can

In bowl mix shrimp, tomatoes, jalapeno, cilantro and pineapple. If you can afford the extra calories add avocado chunks. Serve chilled.

Dinner: Pork Tenderloin in Apricot Glaze, Carrots, Green Beans with Almonds, Mashed Potatoes.

Pork Tenderloin in Apricot Glaze Recipe: One pound of Pork Tenderloin makes 4 servings. You can use leftover pork in a lunch salad of mixed greens, dried cranberries or cherries and orange sections with Lemon Maple Dressing from Day 8.

Preheat oven to 425 F. if not grilling pork

For each 1 pound Pork Tenderloin:
½ tsp. ground ginger
½ tsp. ground allspice
¼ tsp. ground cloves
1/8 tsp. cayenne pepper
½ cup Apricot preserves (preferably a 100% fruit version) or can puree canned apricots
1 Tbsp. Dark Rum (optional)
1 tsp. olive oil if not grilling

In small bowl mix ginger, allspice, cloves and cayenne pepper. Rub spice mixture evenly over pork. Try to do this several hours before cooking. Refrigerate until ready to cook.

In another small bowl mix apricot preserves and rum (optional). Brush apricot mixture over pork just before cooking.

To grill sear the tenderloin on the hottest part of the grill for about 2 minutes each side. Then cook over indirect heat for 10 to 15 more minutes (not turning) until meat thermometer inserted into thickest part registers 160° F being careful to not overcook. Remove from grill, tent with foil and let rest 5 minutes prior to serving.

If not grilling heat 1 tsp. olive oil in skillet over medium high heat. Cook pork in skillet until all sides are browned, about 2 to 3 minutes per side. Place pork on foil lined or lightly oiled baking pan. Bake at 425°, basting once with apricot sauce, for 15 minutes or until meat thermometer inserted into thickest part registers 160° F.   Remove from oven and baste with sauce again.   Tent pork with foil and let rest 5 minutes prior to serving.

Cut in to medallions and serve with remaining sauce.

Carrots and Green Beans: If grilling the pork then mix ½ cup sliced carrots and ½ cup green beans with 1 tsp. olive oil per person. Wrap vegetables in aluminum foil and cook on grill. I like to make individual packets of vegetables for each person or you can do them all together. Garnish carrots and green beans with 1 Tbsp. sliced almonds per person. If not grilling then sauté carrots and green beans in olive oil or prepare however you like.

Mashed Potatoes Recipe:

For every 5 servings:
2 large Potatoes
8 garlic cloves, peeled
2 tsp. olive oil
2 Tbsp. buttermilk (may substitute regular milk, almond or other non dairy milk)
¼ tsp. sea salt
black pepper to taste

Wash potatoes, peel if desired and cut in to small chunks. In a large pot cover potatoes and garlic with water and boil until tender. Drain and return potatoes and garlic to dry pot.   Stir over low heat until any excess water evaporates.   Add olive oil and buttermilk to potatoes and garlic and mash with potato masher until desired consistency.   Add more buttermilk if needed.   Mix in salt and pepper. Serve.

INDEX

Made in the USA
Lexington, KY
05 August 2016